MODERN TAILORING FOR WOMEN

THE MACMILLAN COMPANY
NEW YORK · BOSTON · CHICAGO · DALLAS
ATLANTA · SAN FRANCISCO

MACMILLAN AND CO., Limited
LONDON · BOMBAY · CALCUTTA · MADRAS
MELBOURNE

THE MACMILLAN COMPANY
OF CANADA, Limited
TORONTO

MODERN TAILORING

FOR WOMEN

FRANCES F. MAUCK, M.A.

Associate Professor of Home Economics,

The Ohio State University

THE MACMILLAN COMPANY · NEW YORK

PREFACE

This book has been written for use in schools and colleges where work in the special field of tailoring is offered; for use as a laboratory manual in trade and technical schools; for use by home-makers to whom no other source of help need be available.

Only fundamental processes are included; they do not go out of date. Therefore the application of them may vary with the current fashion. Many processes included may be applied to garments other than the strictly tailored ones mentioned. Since methods for certain construction processes vary among tailors and among teachers, the directions often suggest more than one method.

For effective use of this book, the student or home-maker should read the suggestions offered in the section, "Aids to Following Directions."

The author wishes to express her appreciation to Evelyn Alice Mansfield, Associate Professor of Textiles, Clothing and Related Arts, Michigan State College, for her searching and helpful criticisms; to Mrs. Beatrice M. Walker who shared the work of improving the directions for use in the classroom; and to Mrs. Marjorie Smith Davison who prepared the drawings.

Frances Mauck

Columbus, Ohio

TABLE OF CONTENTS

MODERN TAILORING FOR WOMEN

TYPES OF TAILORING

A distinction should be made among the different types of tailoring, for the directions in this book adhere closely to one type called custom tailoring.

Custom tailoring is done by an individual tailor who is a specialist and a highly skilled craftsman in his field. Usually, he works either in men's wear or in women's wear, but not in both. The planning of the design and the selection of the fabric are matters of personalized service by the tailor, though the customer may take design and fabric to him and ask to have a garment made. Individual measurements are taken and fittings given. The product involves much skilled handwork. Findings are selected for the individual garment and they are of superior quality. Custom tailoring carries a high initial cost, but the customer receives individuality of design and fit and a high degree of durability of shape.

A second type of tailoring also is made-to-order, but in this case it is factory work. The work is both made-to-order and made-to-measure. A retail store usually handles the customer and takes the measurements. The design is selected from a book of available designs. There are no fittings until the finished garment is delivered to the store and to the customer, when alterations may be found necessary. There is less handwork on such products. The price is medium, certainly lower than that for custom tailoring.

A third type is the factory-made garment which is made with no one purchaser in mind. The finished garment is selected at the retail store and refitted, if necessary. The price of such garments is less than that of either of the two types above, for comparable quality of products.

The coat tailored at home may be of the custom type. Instructions in this book are limited to such work except in the discussions of the unlined jacket and children's coats. The coat may be of the dressmaker type, which is a combination of tailoring and dressmaking. After experience in custom tailoring and in dressmaking, it is easy to apply knowledge and skill to a dressmaking type of tailoring.

1

SUPPLIES AND EQUIPMENT

SUPPLIES FOR A TAILORED COAT OR JACKET

Wool fabric.

Lining fabric.

Reinforcement fabric for body of coat, such as wigan or hymo.

Silesia for pocket pouches and for reinforcing buttonholes.

Undercollar fabric, such as melton, if coat fabric is not used.

Linen canvas for reinforcing collar.

Cotton felt for shaping around lower curves of armscye.

Cotton or wool batting and sheet wadding for shoulder padding.

Tape, straight grain, preferably linen, 3/8" wide for staying creaseline, lapel, and front edges. Good quality twill tape may be used for creaseline.

Wigan for stays under mouthlines of pockets.

Sewing silk.

Buttonhole twist.

Gimp or heavy thread for reinforcing worked buttonholes.

Buttons.

Button thread.

EQUIPMENT FOR TAILORING

Sewing machine of the usual type for home use.

Shears of medium size, well sharpened.

Scissors with fine, firm points, well sharpened.

Needles for handwork: #7 sharps for ordinary work, #7 betweens for padding stitch and felling.

Beeswax.

Pressing tools: Board, cushions, and iron, as suggested under "Pressing," pages 106–108.

Tailor's chalk.

Wax chalk.

2

Most of the supplies and equipment listed are available in department stores. Sometimes a saleswoman will not be familiar with a tailor's term such as hymo or wigan. If she knows how the item is to be used in a coat, she usually has a similar item or a substitute to suggest.

Cities, even small ones, often have a tailoring supply house which stocks and sells supplies to tailors. It will sell to the student in school or to the home dressmaker.

Tailors who have their own small shop often have supplies which they will sell to the person who wishes to make her own coat. A tailor, either for men's wear or for women's wear, has comparable supplies.

In large cities there are small shops which carry wide assortments of dressmaker findings. These usually include some or all of the necessary supplies for tailoring.

SELECTION OF FABRIC

Because of methods peculiar to tailoring which differ from the methods used in dressmaking, fabric should be carefully selected. All-wool fabric of good quality is desirable.

Some of the more satisfactory fabrics are firm tweed, covert of the heavier quality, firm yet spongy shepherd's check and hound's tooth check, high-grade flannel, firm and good quality basket weave cloth, and a good quality crepe, if the yarn is not very hard-twisted and the fabric is not very smooth and clear in finish. The texture of many of the novelty plaid suitings is often excellent, but the plaid may be difficult to handle in matching the design at seamlines.

In general, the fabrics which are easier to use are the ones that are medium in thickness and sponginess; that have a simple design in the weave, or in a check or stripe; that have yarns and weave soft enough to shrink or take new shape easily without becoming rough or shiny during the pressing. In the latter case, the fabric should not be so soft that it will not hold the shape after the pressing is done. A medium degree of nap on the fabric lessens the tendency to stretch or to fray.

Some qualities that make fabrics difficult to handle are: fine, hard-twisted yarns; close and very firm weave; unnapped, clear finish. Men's wear worsteds and gabardines have these characteristics. It is difficult to see and to follow the yarns of such fabrics during layout and cutting. Also, these fabrics do not shrink and press to shape easily, and pressing tends to leave shiny spots or streaks.

Other fabrics that may be difficult are the extra thick, spongy, and heavily napped ones. Camel's hair coating is of this type. It is hard to follow the threads of the fabric during layout and cutting, and the napped surface may become either rough or shiny during pressing. Also, it is impossible to obtain clear-cut, sharp edges as on lapels, or clear-cut corners as on collars. Machine work, too, offers some difficulty in tension and in keeping one layer of fabric from slipping along another layer.

Large checks, plaids, and broad stripes should be planned and cut so that the design is matched at seamlines. This point requires care, but is not so difficult as it is wasteful of fabric yardage. If plaids or stripes are uneven-sided, the problem of matching colors and design requires thought and time, and a mistake in cutting may be a serious one.

Fabrics which stretch or fray readily are difficult to cut out accurately, and they lose shape especially during fitting.

The less satisfactory fabrics are gabardine, loose-weave tweed or twill, dress weight fabrics, and men's wear worsteds which have hard-twisted yarn, tight weave, and smooth finish.

PREPARATION OF WOOL FABRIC
AND OTHER SUPPLIES

The wool fabric may have been sponged and shrunk at the factory, or it may be treated by the retail store or tailor at the customer's request. The work may be done at home with ordinary pressing equipment.

If the fabric has been sponged and pressed by store or tailor, marking of grainlines occurs afterwards. However, the marking of grainlines may reveal that the sponging process has warped the lines out of position. In that case, the fabric should be pressed again to restore correct grainlines.

If the sponging is to be done at home, do the marking of grainlines before sponging the fabric.

The importance of marking grainlines accurately and of using these markings throughout the work that follows cannot be overemphasized. Correct use of grainlines is essential to satisfactory work in pattern layout, in fitting, finishing, and pressing. It is a "must" for a coat that is to hold its shape throughout the life of the garment. The marking process is tedious, but the worker is repaid for the time and effort by the time saved in later processes, and by the satisfactory qualities of the finished garment.

MARKING WOOL FABRIC

Flaws. Inspect the fabric for flaws. If there are some, mark around each with a basting thread. A wax chalk mark on the wrong side may serve equally well. Flaws may be avoided when the pattern is cut from fabric.

Warp lines. Follow a warp thread and put in a marking basting in three or four places throughout length of fabric. If warp thread cannot be seen, measure an equal distance from the selvage in several places and mark each place. Baste along a series of such marks. Thus there are several warp lines marked, as well as two selvages to serve as guides in cutting fabric.

Filling lines. Straighten each cut end of fabric by pulling out a filling thread and cutting along the line. If doing so should waste much fabric, follow a filling thread near each cut end and put in a marking basting from selvage to

6

selvage. Put in a series of these lines so that they are about eighteen inches apart. If filling thread cannot be seen easily, marking must be done with extreme care, as follows:

Draw a filling thread out near cut end of fabric. Place this line along edge of end of table. Place a selvage along edge of side of table. Be sure fabric lies flat. Measure from drawn thread line and mark at a point eighteen inches from line. Do this in several places. Baste across fabric through the series of marks.

Repeat this method of marking until there is a series of fillingwise basting lines throughout the length of the fabric.

By now the whole length of fabric has been marked off into large blocks or rectangles. Some basting lines are parallel to selvage and some to filling threads, therefore bastings cross each other at right angles. These right-angle lines will be used repeatedly in later work.

PREPARATION FOR SPONGING AND SHRINKING

Cut off selvages along a threadline, for selvages shrink differently from the body of the fabric. The term "selvage" is used hereafter to designate the cut edges left after selvages were removed. These edges are still on a true warpline just as the selvages were.

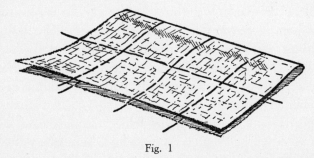

Fig. 1

Fold fabric with right sides facing each other and with selvages coinciding, and with the one half of a fillingwise basting coinciding with the other half (Fig. 1). Pin the two layers of fabric together along this line. Repeat pinning layers of fabric together along each fillingwise basting.

Now the fabric, doubled, is pinned along a series of filling lines. If some sections of fabric between pins are puffy, leave them so and correct them during the next process.

SPONGING AND SHRINKING

There are several methods of treating fabric. Three are suggested here. Whenever the worker checks to see that two lines of basting are at right angles to each other, a tailor's square is an excellent tool. A firm cardboard with a true right-angle corner is satisfactory.

Method 1. With fabric still folded and pinned, lay it on the pressboard so that marking bastings on warplines and filling lines are at right angles. If the board is small, extra care is needed. A padded table top large enough to accommodate the width of fabric is easier to use and may give more satisfactory results.

A dampened cloth laid between two dry cloths is a good press cloth for sponging and shrinking. The dry cloth laid next to the wool fabric prevents too much steam from forming directly on the wool fabric. The dry cloth directly under the iron protects the hand from the possibility of steam burns.

If sections of fabric between pinned lines are puffy, the reason is that some sections were stretched and others were shrunk. To correct puffiness, lay fabric on board with the full side up. Lay press cloths over it. Lower iron against cloths until steam forms and penetrates wool. *Do not* apply pressure. Repeat until the fullness or puffiness is shrunk out. It may be necessary to shrink some puffy sections first on one side of the doubled fabric and then other puffy sections on the other side. Leave the wool slightly moist and then be careful not to wrinkle it as it dries. This process merely shrinks the puffy sections.

To complete the sponging and pressing, lower the warm iron onto the press cloth with some pressure, then lift. Repeat the "press-and-lift" motion until an area of wool is moistened slightly. Repeat throughout length of fabric. Remove pins, a few at a time, just before pressing a pinned section. Press lightly over basting threads. Both pins and bastings may leave press marks on the fabric.

Press upper layer of fabric as it lies folded on pressboard. Work from selvage toward center fold, but *do not* press fold. Turn fabric over and press what was the underlayer.

Remove all remaining pins and unfold fabric.

Lay fabric on board, right side down. Press where the foldline was. Always be careful to see that during pressing the marking bastings remain at right angles. It is wise to check these lines often during the pressing, using a tailor's square or the cardboard with a square corner.

Leave fabric with a slight amount of moisture still in it. Lay it down smoothly and allow it to dry. If, due to lack of space, it is necessary to hang it up, then hang it over a round rod, not a cord or wire, and hang with grainlines straight and true. Shift its position as it dries so that its own weight may not stretch it.

This method requires time and patience, but it produces satisfactory results. A steam iron may be used. With it, the work is done more quickly.

Method 2. Wring a sheet out of warm water. On it lay out the fabric in a single layer, that is, without the usual center fold. Roll the two together loosely so that there are alternate layers of wool and damp sheet. Let stand overnight or several hours.

Remove sheet and place fabric, right side down, on the pressboard. Lay a dry press cloth over the fabric. Lower the warm pressing iron onto the press cloth, then lift. Repeat this "press-and-lift" motion until you have covered the area of fabric which lies with true grainlines on the board.

Check the right angle relationship of warpline and filling line bastings when you lay the fabric on the pressboard, and do so repeatedly.

Press each area of fabric until the entire length is pressed.

Leave the fabric slightly moist and allow it to dry after pressing as in the directions above.

Method 3. This method is used by many tailors. It is quick, easy, and satisfactory, but not all the equipment may be available in home or laboratory.

Dampen thoroughly a sheet or piece of high-grade muslin. The muslin must be pre-shrunk and entirely free from sizing. It should be 4″ to 6″ wider and 18″ longer than the fabric, when the latter is laid out in a single thickness.

Lay wool fabric out smoothly with the grainline markings of warp and filling at right angles to each other. Lay the muslin over the fabric with extra width of muslin placed along each selvage of wool, and with all the extra length of muslin at one end of wool fabric. A large cutting table is helpful, but it is not difficult to do this work on the floor.

Use a board that is 6″ or more longer than the fabric is wide, and that is 10″ or 12″ wide and at least ¾″ thick. A thin board is unsatisfactory. The sharp corners of board should be slightly rounded off or they may leave sharp creases in the fabric. Wrap the muslin and fabric loosely around the board. This wrapping must be done loosely enough so that the fabric may shrink, yet it must be done tightly enough so that, when unrolled, the fabric has no wrinkles. During the process of wrapping, repeatedly check the marking bastings to keep the right-angle relationships; check to see that the markings of filling grainlines lie parallel to the edges of the board.

Allow the rolled fabrics to dry until they are only slightly, very slightly damp. When unrolled, the wool fabric has been sponged, shrunk, and pressed in one operation, and the grainlines are in correct position. A light pressing with a dry press cloth against the wrong side of the fabric restores the finished appearance of the fabric.

PREPARATION OF OTHER SUPPLIES

Shrink reinforcements and tapes by washing them thoroughly in warm water. Let them dry and then press. Wigan is not supposed to shrink, but of recent years this nonshrinking quality has not been dependable.

PATTERN SELECTION AND USE

It is wise to use a commercial pattern for the first tailored garment to be made. These instructions for custom tailoring may be used satisfactorily with such a pattern even though they will differ from those in the pattern instruction sheet. If the worker has had much experience in sewing and designing, she may design her own pattern and use these directions as her sole guide to construction processes.

PATTERN SELECTION

The first garment made by custom tailoring methods should be relatively simple in design so that fitting may not be a major problem, and so that time may be pleasantly spent on the several processes that are different from those in dressmaking. There should be no intricate cuts such as diagonal or deeply curved lines in the seams. On the other hand, it need not be a strictly tailored design, although this type will afford the best experience in learning processes.

In selecting the size of pattern, it is wise to choose one that fits at shoulder and neck, even if alterations must be made for bust and hip. It is easier to change the size for bust and hip than for shoulder and neck, and the results usually produce a better fitting garment. The "set" of the garment at neck and shoulder is one of the most important factors in producing a good looking coat. It is dependent on both fit and correct treatment during the tailoring processes. In both cases, the work will be more easily and more satisfactorily done when there are no pattern alterations or fitting changes in this area of neckline and shoulder.

PATTERN TESTING

Pin pattern pieces together, being sure to take up the full but exact seam allowance. Try the pattern on the body. Since the armscye tears readily, the sleeve is not pinned in but is tested separately. In a short jacket or fitted coat, it is helpful to mark the waistline of the pattern clearly, adjust it to the

11

waistline of the body, and fit as necessary above and below the waistline.

Cut the complete pattern from medium weight muslin. A worn sheet is satisfactory. Cut it according to grainlines as indicated on the pattern. Baste it together with accuracy. A long, loose stitch on the sewing machine is a quick and satisfactory means of basting.

The muslin model is carefully fitted for several reasons. Fitting changes may cause a difference in the layout of pattern on the more expensive wool fabric. Also, the pattern layout will be fully understood and, in the end, actual timesaving results. Another reason is that there will be fewer and perhaps no fitting changes in the wool garment and the worker may concentrate on tailoring processes. Also, it is easier for the worker and better for the wool fabric to make no fitting changes in the wool. Pockets and buttons may be located in the muslin and, later, made in the wool without having to try the wool garment on. New construction processes, such as pockets, may be tried out on the muslin.

PATTERN ALTERATION

Most commercial jacket and coat patterns will need some alteration. Various textbooks on dress construction and bulletins published by pattern companies give excellent directions for pattern alteration. Although these directions are usually for dress patterns, the same principles apply to jackets and coats. Unless the worker has had some experience in alteration of patterns, she should not undertake to make major changes in a coat pattern.

When the pattern has been chosen for correct fit through the neck and shoulder area, it may be too snug over the bust. Keep the muslin model adjusted to the body at neck, shoulder, and armscye, and keep the center front lines pinned together. Let the seams out as necessary, leaving a smooth curve in the seamlines. If a large amount of change is to be made, it is better to let out the garment in more than one place so that there is only a small change made on any one line. Depending on the design of the pattern, this latter suggestion may or may not be possible to carry out.

Frequently, the pattern is too long-waisted. See that markings for the waistline fall along the waistline of the body and shorten the pattern above this line. This point is important in fitted and semifitted garments.

The hipline area may be snug. Again, be sure that the pattern is adjusted to the waistline before changing the hipline. Let out seams as needed, again making only small amounts of change on any one seamline and leaving smooth curves on all lines.

Another change frequently needed for the average figure is at the shoulder of the back. If the pattern forms a diagonal wrinkle from the shoulder blade toward the underarm, place a short dart from the shoulder seam, vertically toward the shoulder. The dart will change the shoulder seam in position and length, and it may change the position of the armscye line in the back. Restore the original lines of shoulder and armscye line after laying in the dart. Such a dart is often found in coat patterns. In the case of the altered pattern, the wool fabric may be cut with the dart as planned; or the extra length of shoulder seam may be eased in, and then shrunk and pressed until the seam is of the original length.

The sleeve cap may be too short. If it is, diagonal lines fall from the top of the sleeve toward the underarm and the sleeve looks drawn over the forward bone of the shoulder. To lengthen the cap, form a new curved line across the top half of the sleeve and above the original line. This new line graduates into the original line on each side where the pattern notches are.

Frequently during fitting, the only adjustment a sleeve needs is to have the ease or fullness brought forward $\frac{1}{4}''$ to $\frac{1}{2}''$ at the top of the sleeve. The pattern marking showing where the top of sleeve joins the shoulder seam-line is then forward of the shoulder seam.

PATTERN LAYOUT

A soft wood table is most satisfactory to use in layout and cutting. The fabric may be laid out with a filling line along one end of table and a warp-line along an edge, and these lines may be pinned to the table. Pinning along true grainlines and edges of table ensures an accurate beginning, and provides a means of maintaining position of fabric.

If fabric is laid on the table wrong side up, the problem of markings will be simplified. When fabric is doubled for the layout, lay the right sides together so that wrong sides are on the outside.

The warp and filling grainlines must be checked repeatedly so that the one is at right angles to the other, and so that they lie parallel to the end and the edge of table, respectively. A tailor's square is a good tool to use, for warplines and filling lines should follow the right-angle arms of the square. If one is not available, a large square or rectangle of cardboard may be used, though one edge must be exactly at right angles to another edge. If the checking is accurate, the filling thread at each end of the fabric will be found to be at right angles to the warp.

When fabric is doubled in order to lay out a part of the pattern, the grain-lines of fabric should be checked most carefully. Warplines of the upper layer of fabric must coincide with those of the underlayer; filling lines of the upper layer must coincide with those of the underlayer.

If there is a nap on the fabric, the pattern pieces should all be laid in one direction so that the downward line of a pattern piece runs in the same direction as the downward direction of the nap. Even if there is no obvious nap of fabric, it is best to lay the pattern on in this same way, all pieces in one direction.

When the pattern markings for warp grainlines are laid on warp grainline of fabric, *pin pattern to fabric along this line first*. Then pattern should not slip during the rest of pinning.

If it is difficult to see which is the right and which is the wrong side of the fabric, place an occasional "X" with chalk on the wrong side of fabric throughout its length. When pattern is removed, be sure there is a chalk mark on each cut piece of fabric.

PATTERN CUTTING

Tailors usually cut off all seam edges on patterns, lay out the pieces on the fabric so as to allow for seam edges, and then chalkmark around each pattern piece. This method is quick and accurate in giving a clean-cut line for seams. Chalk should be sharpened to a thin edge.

If pattern has been laid on doubled fabric, do not cut through both layers at once. This is especially important with heavy wools. Cut the top layer and then the underlayer of fabric. The extra time necessary is repaid by the accuracy of cutting.

If there is a decided nap on the fabric, cut from the top end of the pattern piece toward the bottom end. This direction of cutting is easier and tends to leave a truer line on cut edge.

Do not cut the notches on seamlines either inward or outward. Cut straight along the seam edge. Mark the notches later.

PATTERN MARKING

Mark notches with chalk, using the wax chalk so that the markings will not rub off before you need to use them. Tailor tacks may be used, though care must be taken to prevent the threads from falling out before markings are used. Also, they should be removed before machine stitching crosses them.

Be sure that the center front line on each piece of the front, the center back line, the warpline and filling line of sleeve cap are transferred to the fabric.

The pattern will indicate warplines, but not usually the filling lines. Draw a filling line on sleeve pattern at right angles to the warpline.

If seam edges of the pattern were cut off and pattern edges were outlined with chalk, the marking of seamlines has been done. If seam edges were left on the pattern, thread marks should be put in along the stitching lines of the seams. This is a tedious process but accuracy of seamlines is important. When thread marks are used, remove them before machine stitching these lines, so that the machine stitch will not catch them securely and make them hard to remove.

Thread marks and tailor tacks are satisfactory for transferring perforation markings to fabric. Thread marks are quickly made but they pull out readily and therefore are only temporary. Chalk may be used, but it must be remembered that the wax type leaves a mark that may be difficult to remove and the other type leaves a mark that may rub off too soon.

Another quick method is to use tracing paper with a tracing wheel. Such paper is usually available in colors so that the best color for a particular fabric may be used. Some regular carbon papers leave a mark that is difficult to remove. Therefore markings made with them should not be placed where they will show in the finished garment.

If all chalk or carbon markings are on the wrong side of the fabric, these cautions about difficulty of removing the marks may be disregarded. For seams and darts, it is satisfactory to mark the wrong side. The right side should be marked for pocket, button, and buttonhole positions. Thread marks or tailor tacks are then desirable.

FABRIC DESIGN IN LAYOUT AND CUTTING

When the fabric has a decided design, such as a plaid or stripe, there are two points to consider in layout and cutting. One is the placement of the design so that it falls on a certain part of the body when the garment is worn. The important lines are the center front; center back; the line which runs across the chest width, back width, and the top of sleeve; the ends of collar; and the outer edge of lapel facing. Often the center of a stripe or plaid becomes the center front and center back lines of the coat. The pattern is laid on the fabric so that these centers of design and of coat pattern coincide. Later, they will fall along the center lines of the body. Also, the edge of a stripe or plaid may follow the width-of-chest line and line across the top of the sleeve. In the latter case, the design is matched at the armscye seamline. The outer edge of lapel facing is often laid along the lengthwise grain of a striped fabric in order to avoid the awkward bias lines of stripes along this facing edge.

Matching designs at seamlines is the second point to consider in layout and cutting. Instruction sheets of commercial patterns offer help on matching designs at seamlines, but the suggestions here may provide additional help. After deciding where the design should fall in relation to the body, place the pattern on the fabric so as to carry out this decision. Trace the design of the fabric on to the paper pattern along the seamlines where the design is to be matched. Be sure that this tracing indicates where the *stitching* line of the seam cuts across the design of the fabric. The stitching line is more important than is the edge of the paper pattern. If the design is intricate and perhaps multi-colored, colored crayons may be used to mark the paper pattern or the names of the colors may be written on the pattern.

The next step is to lay the second piece of paper pattern onto the first, pinning the two together accurately along the stitching line of the seam, which will later join the two pieces of fabric. Mark the second piece of pattern, again along the *stitching* line of the seam, transferring the line and color markings from the first to the second piece of the paper pattern.

Last, lay this second piece of pattern onto the fabric so that the markings on the paper pattern fall on identical lines and colors of the fabric.

In basting and stitching the seams where design of fabric is matched, the basting should be carefully done. It is wise to pin along these lines before basting, checking to see that the design is still matched. Insert pins at right angles to seamlines. After basting and fitting and before machine stitching the seams, pins should be inserted again so that one layer of fabric cannot slip along the other layer thus leaving the design inaccurately matched. Pins are removed as stitching is done.

Another method of ensuring that the designs continue to match during basting and stitching is to pin the seamline as a lapped seam and then slip baste from the right side. When ready to stitch insert pins again, as in paragraph above, to prevent slipping during the stitching.

The vertical line of the center back of the collar usually looks like a continuation of the design of the center back of the coat. The line across the width-of-chest line and top of sleeve often gives the effect of an unbroken design. This point is especially true with plaids. When stripes are matched at the armscye seamline, the effect may be one of the points directed upward.

The design at ends of collar should be planned in relation to the lines of design in lapels. In a striped fabric, the stripes may form an interesting angle where lapel and collar are joined along the gorgeline.

Frequently there is confusion as to the correct layout for cutting twilled fabrics. Twills have only a right and wrong side. There is no up and down. Therefore, the only consideration in layout and cutting is to see that twills are cut for a right and wrong side, just as is a cotton print which has no up and down effect in the design.

AIDS TO FOLLOWING DIRECTIONS

This book is prepared with the belief that a person who has had some experience in sewing but none in tailoring can read these directions, follow them with understanding, and make a coat satisfactory to herself. The directions are planned for use with a commercial pattern. They may be used as a supplement to the pattern instruction sheet, or as the only help needed in making a coat.

To be most effective, directions for any one process should be read carefully from beginning to end while the reader is trying to visualize each step of procedure. Sketches should be studied during the reading.

The next step is to begin the process under consideration and to proceed, step by step, according to directions. No detail of work should be omitted or slighted. The worker should not jump to conclusions and complete a step unless the directions so indicate. If a point is not clear, stop the work and read ahead. Frequently, later directions will clear up the point of confusion.

As far as possible, the instructions for each process are organized under three headings: Cutting, Marking, and Construction. The paragraphs on cutting found in each division should be read before cutting any of the garment. Likewise, all paragraphs on marking should be read before markings are completed. The directions for construction need to be read in detail only when the worker is ready to begin a certain process.

The order of topics is the order in which a coat or jacket may be made. It follows the same sequence as that suggested in "Order of Procedure in Making a Coat," page 20.

In selecting a commercial pattern to be used with this text, the design should be one that is suitable for developing in custom tailoring. The chief point to avoid is softness or drapiness of design, although custom tailoring is not limited to severely tailored lines.

The instruction sheet that accompanies the commercial pattern is helpful, although most such instructions are not for true custom tailoring. They should be compared with the directions presented here.

The list of supplies needed for the particular design may be checked against the list given in this book.

Pattern directions may suggest unbleached muslin as reinforcement for the coat front, but hymo or similar fabric should be used as suggested in this list; in preparation of fabric and in layout and cutting, the directions given here will supplement or improve upon the pattern directions.

The figures in the drawings show a jacket with a side gore, called a body gore, for many commercial patterns have a similar gore. Therefore, the jacket in these drawings has a front, a body gore and a back. If the pattern selected by the worker has only a front and back piece, the worker should remember that her side seamline will fall in a line that will compare to a center line of the body gore in the drawings.

ORDER OF PROCEDURE IN MAKING A COAT

Tailors and other coat makers differ as to the best order of procedure. Whatever order is followed, it should be one that is well planned, so that each step is completed by the time it is needed as a basis for the next step

An order of the steps in making a coat is suggested here, though it may vary with the design of the garment and with the preference of the worker. Some workers prefer to baste the sleeves into the coat for the first fitting, as in the order listed below. Some prefer to fit the body of the coat and then pin the sleeves into position during the first fitting. In the latter case, the following procedure may be used, omitting the basting in of sleeves for the first fitting, and following the suggestions below for pinning sleeves into position during the first fitting.

PREPARATION FOR FIRST FITTING

1. Coat is completely basted together with shaped reinforcement in place. Check to see that edges have been taped as they should be.
2. No facings are applied for first fitting.
3. Collar is basted on with lapped raw edges at seamlines.
4. Grainlines, button positions, lapel creaselines, pocket lines, and decorative features are marked.
5. Shoulder pads must be in coat, even if they are only semimade.
6. Sleeves are basted in, or they may be pinned into place during this fitting.
7. Hem of coat is basted in place.
8. If the coat is to be belted, have a belt of the correct width.

FIRST FITTING

1. Check general lines and proportions of silhouette.
2. Check spacing of all areas including decorative features.
3. Check center front and center back warplines and filling threads at chestline and bustline in front and at width-of-back line.

 4. Check position and direction of seams and darts.
 5. Check neck and shoulder line. (See "Seams," p. 56.)
 6. Check collar.
 7. Check creaseline of collar and of lapel to see that they meet.
 8. Check line of lap of front edges.
 9. Check sleeves as to length, width, grainlines, if they were basted in.
10. Check length of coat.
11. Check details:
    a. roll of lapels
    b. position and size of buttons
    c. position and size of pockets
    d. wrist finish
12. Pin sleeves into place, if they were not basted in for this fitting.

PROCEDURE AFTER FIRST FITTING

1. Remove sleeves whether they were basted or pinned for the first fitting.
2. Mark changes made in first fitting. Make right and left sides alike.
3. Make alterations and recheck.

PREPARATION FOR SECOND FITTING

 1. Stitch darts and press.
 2. Shape front and back on cheese block or ham cushion.
 3. Make pockets and press them. Reshape coat front, if necessary.
 4. Fit and shape reinforcement.
 5. Baste in reinforcement of front.
 6. Make padding stitch in lapel.
 7. Make bound buttonholes now, if their position is correct.
 8. Baste reinforcement into back.
 9. Baste side seams and shoulder seams.
10. Turn up hem.
11. Finish shoulder pads and place in position.
12. Turn front edges and lapel edges back and baste. (No facings.)
13. Stitch front sleeve seam, if sleeve was fitted satisfactorily in first fitting.
14. Baste in sleeves.

SECOND FITTING

Check each item handled in the preparation for this fitting.

PROCEDURE AFTER SECOND FITTING

1. Take coat apart, where necessary.
2. Make bound buttonholes in outer layer of coat fabric, if they were not previously made.
3. Put edge tape on lapel edge and creaseline.
4. Put on front facings. Finish bound buttonholes on facing side.
5. Put edge finish such as hand stitching on lapel.
6. Stitch body seams. Press.
7. Stitch shoulder seams. Press.
8. Lap raw seam edges of reinforcement along shoulder and underarm seams. Catstitch these seams.
9. Put in shoulder pads but do not fully fasten them to the coat. They are removed when sleeves are being stitched into the armscye.
10. Collar:
    a. Attach undercollar to coat.
    b. Shape topcollar.
    c. Put on topcollar.
11. Finish sleeves and line them. Replace sleeves in coat. Stitch and press armscye seam.
12. Hem:
    a. Insert reinforcement.
    b. Finish.
13. Make worked buttonholes.
14. Press.
15. Put in lining.
16. Sew buttons on coat.
17. Give final light pressing.

TAPING

Taping of lapel and coat front is explained in the section on lapel, pages 48–49.

Other taping is done as soon as coat is cut out, in order to prevent stretching of edges. Some of the tape remains in the finished coat. If it does remain, it is usually held in place by the stitching of the seamlines. Some of the tape may be removed as soon as fitting is finished and seams are stitched.

Places to be taped. Tape the neckline across back of neck; armscye line; side seamline; often, the shoulder seamline.

How to apply tape. Place one edge of tape on the seam where stitching will be done. Other edge of tape lies toward the body of the coat and *not* on the seam allowance. Baste in place with even basting. These threads will be removed later.

When to apply tape and when to remove it. Apply to back of neckline as soon as fabric is cut out. A line of machine stitching may be used here, instead of tape. Remove when collar has been fitted and undercollar is attached. Apply to each section of armscye line as soon as fabric is cut out. The tape on each section of armscye is removed later when the lower curve of each is held in with a taut thread and pressed to shape. Then the tape is replaced so as to hold the armscye in its new position. If, during fittings, the armscye seamline is changed, the tape should be changed so that the edge still falls on the line for stitching the armscye line.

Apply only to one side of shoulder seam and to one side of side seam. If there are darts or seams that run into these seams, they may be basted in before the tape is applied. The untaped side of the shoulder and side seams should be carefully pinned and basted to the taped side, for the former may stretch in the process of making the seam. If the fabric is loosely woven or stretchy, these tapes should be held permanently in place by the stitching on the seam lines. If the fabric is nonstretchy and is bulky, the stitching of seams should not catch the tape. The tape is removed after the stitching is done.

23

The tape may have to be clipped or darted to adjust it to curved seamlines or around a corner.

The free edge of tape remains free and so is not fastened to the wool fabric.

TREATMENT OF DARTS IN WOOL FABRICS

Treatment after stitching depends on width of dart and texture of fabric. For pressing darts, see general directions under "Pressing," pages 106–111.

Very narrow darts. Do not cut open. Press folded edge in desired direction. Be careful that this bulky line does not show a mark on the right side, due to overpressing.

Narrow darts (1). Depending on width of dart and texture of fabric, dart may be pressed to form a small box pleat without cutting open any part of the dart.

Narrow darts (2). Some narrow darts may be cut open to a point within 1″ to 1½″ of the pointed end. Press open the cut edges. Press the inch or so which is not cut, so as to form a tiny box pleat.

Wide darts. Cut open as far toward the point as reasonable, perhaps ¼″ from the end. Treat as "Narrow Darts (2)" above.

Very wide darts. Cut open, trim to correct width and treat as "Wide Darts."

Curved darts. If possible, these should be cut open and cut edges clipped so that they will lie flat after pressing.

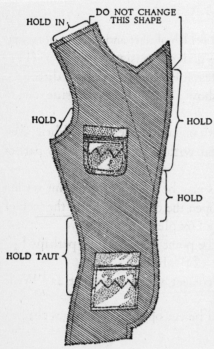

HOLD IN

DO NOT CHANGE
THIS SHAPE

HOLD

HOLD

HOLD

HOLD TAUT

Fig. 2

Baste, stitch, and press darts. See instructions for "Treatment of Darts," page 25.

Follow directions shown with Fig. 2 "Shaping Coat Front." Use a taut thread with fine running stitches for places to be held in. Remove tape wherever a section of fabric is to be held in. Replace tape after the shaping is done.

The shaped front must be handled even more carefully than the shaped reinforcement since it may stretch more readily.

Be especially careful about the shaping at the lower curve of the armscye. If this is well done, the coat will fit better, will hold its shape better, and will be more comfortable during wear. To shape the curve, put in a fine running stitch along the armscye seam line, from the side seam to a point just above the notch marking. Draw up this thread by ⅜". Fasten the thread ends firmly so that they will not yield during the pressing and shaping.

The reinforcement will be darted and pressed at a point corresponding to the place where the wool is held in. See page 42, "Reinforcement of the Body of the Coat, Fitting" and Fig. 7. The layer of cotton felt around the front armscye of the reinforcement will be treated so as to supplement the "holding in" of the wool and the darting of the reinforcement.

During pressing to shape, use the ham cushion for curved areas such as those of the bust (Fig. 65).

SHAPING COAT BACK

Sometimes there is no special shaping in addition to that which results from the use of darts. Frequently, the lower curve of the back armscye needs to be held in, just as the lower curve of the front armscye is held in. The process is the same for both curves. The amount may be less than in front.

The possible need for the shaping of the armscye should be looked for during the first fitting. It is as important to correct fit, to maintenance of shape, and to comfort as is the shaping of the front armscye line.

POCKETS

Three types of pockets are presented below. They are the three most commonly used in coats and jackets of the custom-made type. See page 127 for discussion of patch pockets. It is easy to work out variations of each of these types after the basic type is fully understood.

Among tailors there are minor differences of procedure and of technique in making any one type of pocket. To simplify directions, only one order of procedure and usually only one technique are suggested here.

Terms used for parts of a pocket vary so much that a few are defined below as they are used in the following instructions:

Mouthline, the opening through which the hand passes in order to use the pocket.

Pocket linings, the pieces which are attached to the opening of a pocket so as to form the pouch.

Upper pocket lining, the lining piece which lies next to the outside of the coat.

Under pocket lining, the lining piece which lies next to the lining of the coat. These two definitions of upper and under pocket linings should be carefully noted. "Upper" and "under" respectively, indicate that the lining is nearer to and farther from the outside of the coat.

Stay, a strip of reinforcement fabric laid against the wrong side of the coat, under the mouthline.

Pocket facing, a piece of wool usually attached to a piece of pocket lining so that the wool, not the lining, will show when the pocket is in use.

Welt, of a welt pocket, the only portion that shows from the right side of the coat when the pocket is completed.

Welt, of a flap pocket, a narrow strip of wool, similar to a binding, that finishes one edge of the mouthline. It does not show when the flap is in position. One edge of the mouthline is finished with the flap, the other edge with a welt.

FLAP POCKET

A flap pocket may be placed straight or slightly slanted on the coat. It is usually slanted, because a coat tends to dip toward the front.

The shape of the flap is determined by the style of the coat. A straight flap looks well on a double-breasted coat, but a rounded end looks better on a single-breasted coat. The shape of the front corners of the coat affect the design of the flap.

MARKING

Use marking basting with colored thread. Thin-edged chalk and ruler may be used first to make a straight line.

Mark mouthline on coat front. The marking line extends at least 1″ beyond each end of length of flap.

Mark each end of flap with guide basting at right angles to mouthline (Fig. 3a).

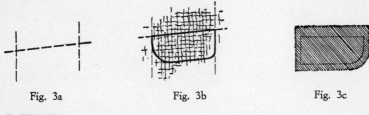

Fig. 3a   Fig. 3b   Fig. 3c

CUTTING

Cut the flap from coat fabric, matching the grainline to the grainline of the coat. Match design of fabric such as stripes, unless flap is purposely cut with a contrast of design (Fig. 3b).

Allow 1/8″ seams at bottom and ends, 1/2″ at top (Fig. 3c).

Cut flap lining from lining fabric, exactly like the flap.

Cut welt of coat fabric, ends on warpwise grain, 1½″ wide and 1″ longer than pocket.

Cut pocket facing exactly like welt. This may be wool or of lining fabric.

Cut two pieces of pocket lining from silesia or similar material 2″ wider than the flap is long and as deep as desired. The finished pouch to be formed from the two pieces of pocket lining should be at least 1″ shorter than the distance from the pocket mouthline to the hem of the jacket. In other words, the pocket pouch should not lap over the hem of the jacket.

Cut a stay of wigan or silesia lengthwise of grain 1½″ wide and 2″ longer than the flap. Wigan results in a slightly stiffer pocket than does silesia.

CONSTRUCTION

Each step in construction should be followed by pressing.

A. *Prepare the flap*. Two methods are suggested here. By following either set of directions, the lining of flap will prove to be somewhat smaller than the wool flap so that, when turned and pressed, the seam will not show from the right side.

Method 1. This method is especially good in a case where the design of the fabric in flap and in body of coat should be matched, as with stripes or plaid.

Cut flap from wool according to size and shape desired.

Use wool flap as a pattern for cutting lining.

Lay the two pieces, right sides together, and tailor baste lengthwise through center of flap (Fig. 3d).

Pull wool back about ⅟₁₆″ from each of the three edges to be stitched, namely, the ends and lower edge. Use fine tailor basting near the raw edges to hold the wool in this position (Fig. 3d).

Fig. 3d

Stitch ⅛″ from raw edge of wool across the two ends and the lower line of flap. The upper edge of flap is not stitched. Stitch with *wool side down* on the machine.

Trim seam edges. Turn right side out, finger press, baste, and press lightly.

Method 2. Lay flap and lining, with right sides together, and place under presser foot of machine with lining side up. Do not baste. While stitching, the lining will slip away from the wool flap and seemingly become longer.

Stitch across one end, around one corner of the flap, and about 2″ along the length of the flap. This has made the lining longer.

Stop stitching and leave needle inserted.

Trim away the excess lining across the unstitched end and around the corner to make the lining the same size as the wool. The excess is about ⅛″. Complete the stitching around second corner and the end. The upper edge of flap is not stitched.

Trim seam edges, turn and press as in Method 1.

Edgestitching is optional. If used, sew through lining as well as through fabric.

B. *Prepare the two pieces of pocket lining*. Lay pocket facing, which is either wool or lining fabric, centered on one piece of pocket lining, both with

right sides up. Raw edges of facing and
lining are matched. Zigzag over the
lower raw edge of wool facing or turn
this edge under and edgestitch, Fig. 3e.

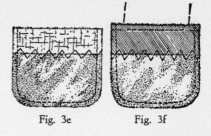

Lay wool welt centered on the other
piece of pocket lining, both with right
sides up. Raw edges of welt and lining
are matched. Zigzag over the lower raw
edge of wool welt, or turn under this edge and edgestitch. The upper edge
of this pocket lining may be cut away so that there is only the one layer of
wool left along the upper part of the lining. Fig. 3f shows this lining and
welt from the wrong side.

The preparation of these two pieces of pocket lining is the same, except
that you have a choice of fabric for the pocket facing.

C. *Attach stay and welt to mouthline of pocket.* Pin pocket
stay under the mouthline, against the wrong side of the
coat. Center the stay on the mouthline. The placement of
the stay is shown in Fig. 3k with the completed pocket.

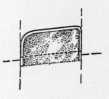

Place pocket welt (including lining) on *lower* side of
pocket mouthline, centered on the mouthline. With right
sides together, plan for $\frac{1}{8}''$ seam measuring from the

Fig. 3g

mouthline. Bulky fabrics require more than $\frac{1}{8}''$. Stitch this seam so that
each end is $\frac{1}{8}''$ short of mouthline as marked. Backstitch each end (Fig. 3h).

D. *Attach flap and welt to mouthline of pocket.* Mark
lengthwise of flap with thread on the *lining side* of flap
as a guide line for $\frac{1}{2}''$ seams. Place this marked line
of flap along upper edge of mouthline, right sides of
coat and flap together, and flap upside down. Allow
$\frac{1}{8}''$ seam on pocket mouthline. Stitch on basting line
from end to end of flap, backstitching at ends (Figs.
3g–3h).

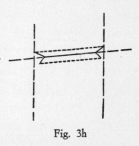

Fig. 3h

E. *Cut pocket mouthline.* Cut only fabric of the coat and pocket stay.

Cut along pocket mouthline, cutting short of each end by $\frac{3}{8}''$
to $\frac{1}{2}''$.

Cut diagonally to the end of the stitching of the flap and stitching of the
welt so as to leave long triangles at each end. Note that the triangles at the
ends are not even-sided, because the stitching of the flap is longer than the
stitching of the welt by $\frac{1}{8}''$ at each end (Fig. 3h).

E. *Press welt seam open.* In pressing, leave pocket lining on outside of coat and draw lining toward top of coat. Press from wrong side.

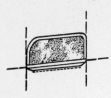

Turn pocket lining to wrong side of coat and form a welt ¼″ wide or less. On the right side of the coat, this wool welt is first turned upward toward the pocket mouthline; then on the wrong side, it is turned downward so that its folded edge enclosed the edge of the seam which has been pressed open. Stitch

Fig. 3i

exactly in the line of the seam between welt and coat. The welt should not crowd the flap (Fig. 3i).

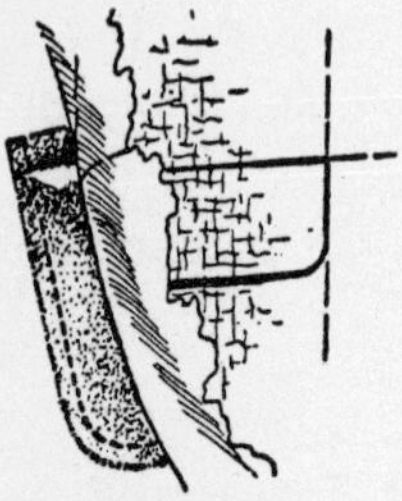

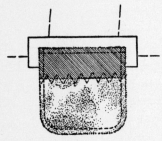

G. *Baste seam where flap and coat are joined, so that all seam edges turn upward.* Inaccuracy in this step may cause the flap to stand out away from the coat when the pocket is completed.

H. *Fold coat and pocket stay.* With welt and flap in position, fold coat and pocket stay back until triangle at end

Fig. 3j

of mouthline is visible from the wrong side of coat. Backstitch across base of triangle. Repeat at other end of mouthline (Fig. 3j).

I. *Place pocket lining.* Place with its wool facing toward the mouthline and with its upper edge along the upper raw edge of flap. Stitch lining and facing to edge of flap and stay. This is done from the wrong side of the coat (Fig. 3k).

J. *Backstitch.* Backstitch across ends of mouthline from the right side. A bar tack may

Fig. 3k

be used here.

K. *Stitch pocket linings together and form a pouch.* (Fig. 3k).

L. *Press.*

WELT POCKET

This pocket is often located as indicated in Fig. 4a. The position varies with style and proportions of garment. The welt should slant downward toward the front, even though it may appear to be on the horizontal. The amount of slant depends on the figure.

The welt shown in Fig. 4c has one end on warp grain. One end is curved. The end on warp grain is placed toward the armscye line. This end matches the grain of fabric of coat. The design of fabric also is matched.

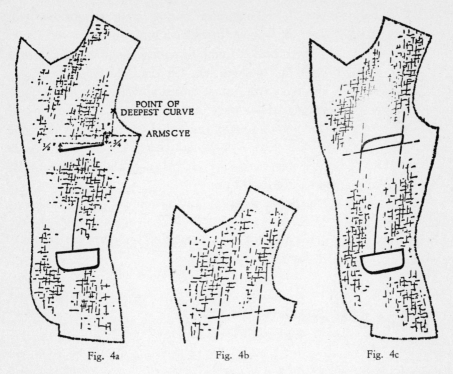

Fig. 4a Fig. 4b Fig. 4c

MARKING

Mark position of mouthline with basting. This basting should extend 1″ or more beyond each end of mouthline. Mark each end of mouthline with a basting on warp grainline (Fig. 4b).

CUTTING

Wool welt. Cut to follow the grain and design of coat fabric at the position marked on the coat. Good dimensions for a finished welt are ⅞″ high and 3¾″ long, but these vary with style and proportion of the coat. Make ½″ seam allowance on all sides and mark seam lines with chalk. Remember that one end is a straight warpline and one end is curved (Figs. 4d, 4e).

Fig. 4d Fig. 4e

Welt reinforcement. Use wigan with top edge on selvage. Cut with ¼″ seam allowance on mouthline, but with no seam allowances on the other three sides. Shape the corners according to the corners of welt (Fig. 4e).

Pocket stay. Use wigan cut on lengthwise grain, 2″ wide and 2″ longer than the welt.

Pocket linings. Use silesia or lining material. There are two pieces for pocket linings, one for the upper and one for the underlining. The under-lining has a wool facing.

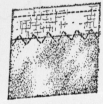

Cut upper lining with sides on warp grain, and use the welt as a guide for shaping the top. The width is at least 1″ more than the length of mouthline (Fig. 4f).

Cut underlining with sides on warp grain and use mouthline on coat as guide for cutting slant of upper edge. The width is at least 1″ more than the length of mouthline. The depth or length is about ½″ more than the length of the upper lining.

Fig. 4f   Fig. 4g

Cut wool facing to be attached to underlining, using the underlining as the guide. Cut it 1½″ to 2″ wide (Fig. 4g).

CONSTRUCTION

A. *Prepare the welt and upper lining.* Lay wigan reinforcement against wrong

Fig. 4h

side of wool welt. It lies inside of the seam allowances of wool welt, except at lower edge where wool seam allow-ance is ½″ and wigan seam allowance is ¼″. Selvage is at the upper edge. Tailor baste the two together. This basting is not removed until the coat is finished (Fig. 4h).

Gather around the two top corners of the welt ⅜″ from raw edge with double thread of matching color, using very fine stitches. Run these gathers about ¼″ along each side of each corner (Fig. 4h). Tighten the gathers to make the wool fold over the welt reinforcement. Cut out excess material at the corners by cutting out dart-shaped pieces, like notches, almost to the gathering thread. Do not cut a notch exactly at the corner, but at each side of the corner.

Fold edge of wool over and baste ends and upper edge of welt. Skip over the gathered corners with this basting.

Finish welt at gathered corners, using yarns pulled from the fabric to bring raw edges of clipped notches together. The corners of the welt, when finished, should be smoothly rounded.

Catstitch raw edge of ends and upper edge of welt to wigan. Press on wood (Fig. 4i).

Fig. 4i

Mark stitching line for the mouthline on right side of welt with chalk. Trim to ½″ seam. Mark the stitching line on wrong side also with chalk.

Trim wigan reinforcement so that the lower edge has no seam allowance except for the last ¼″ at each end, where there is extra bulk.

Place upper lining against the welt, wrong sides together, and slipstitch lining to welt across the top and around the corners. Leave ½″ free at each end (Fig. 4j).

B. *Place pocket stay.* Place against wrong side of coat centered on mouthline. Warp line of stay runs in same direction as mouthline. Baste in place. See its placement in the finished pocket in Fig. 4m.

C. *Prepare underlining and facing.* Place wool pocket facing on underlining (silesia) right sides up and mouthlines

Fig. 4j

matching. Zigzag lower edge of wool or turn edge under and topstitch, stitching through wool and lining. Stitch upper raw edges together ⅛″ from edge. Press. (Fig. 4g).

D. *Make the pocket.* Place welt upside down along the lower edge of pocket mouthline, right sides together. Marked seamline of welt is ¼″ below mouthline. Fold lining out of the way. Stitch on marked line, retracing at ends (Fig. 4l).

Place underlining with its wool facing along upper edge of mouthline of coat, right sides together. Edge meets raw edge of welt. Baste for ⅛″ seam, or more for bulky wool (Fig. 4k). Turn welt up into position merely to check length of stitching on underlining. Ends of stitching must fall within the ends of the welt.

Stitch underlining, retracing each end. This second stitching along pocket mouthline should be ⅜″ from the first stitching along mouthline.

Cut through coat and stay along mouthline, leaving a long triangle at each end as with flap pocket.

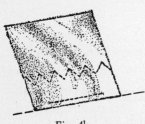

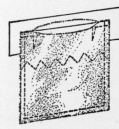

Fig. 4k   Fig. 4l   Fig. 4m

Pull pocket linings through to wrong side. Press open the seam along each side of mouthline, except at the ends. Seam edges at ends of welt *all* turn down. Seam edges at ends of underlining *all* turn up (Fig. 4m). Clip seams to allow them to do so.

Clip welt lining where necessary in order to complete the slipstitching of the lining to the welt and thus finish the ends already started.

Slipstitch lining to welt along the mouthline.

Stitch across the triangles at each end of mouthline and backstitch. Work from wrong side as with flap pocket. Stitch pocket linings to form a pouch. Include the stay in this stitching (Fig. 4m).

Slipstitch ends of welt to coat. Work from the right side. This must be firmly done.

E. *Press.*

SLOT POCKET

Like other pockets, slot pockets have a mouthline formed by a slash or cut in the body of the coat fabric. Each edge of the mouthline is finished by an extra piece of fabric. The pouch is formed by two pieces of pocket lining, which are attached respectively to the pieces that finish the edges of the mouthline.

Variations in the final effect of such pockets is largely dependent on four things. They are: the shape of the mouthline, whether it is a straight or curved line; the width of the strips which finish the edges of the mouth-

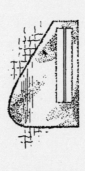
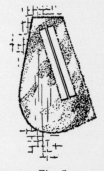

Fig. 5a   Fig. 5b   Fig. 5c

line; the grain of the fabric used in cutting these strips, whether they are warpwise, fillingwise, or bias; and the direction in which the seams along the edges of the mouthline are turned. The last point makes a considerable difference in the appearance of the finished product. The seam edges on the wrong side of the mouthline may be pressed open so that the finished pocket is flush with, or on the same level, as the body of the coat. The seam edges may be pressed toward the mouthline of the pocket so that the edges of the slash appear to be bound and to lie slightly above the surface of the body of the coat. The seam edges may be turned away from the mouthline so that the edges of the slash appear to be piped and thus lie slightly below the surface of the body of the coat.

MARKING

Use marking basting with contrasting thread.

Mark the mouthline on coat front. The marking line extends at least 1″ beyond each end of the planned line of pocket.

Mark each end of mouthline with a basting at right angles to the mouthline (Fig. 5f).

CUTTING

Cut two strips of coat fabric about 2″ wide and 1″ longer than the mouthline of the pocket. If the mouthline is a straight line, the strips may be cut either with the warp, or with the filling or with the true bias running lengthwise of the strip. If the mouthline is curved, these strips should be true bias. For convenience here, these strips will be called binding strips.

Cut a strip of reinforcement fabric, such as wigan, for the stay. It is 1½″ to 2″ wide and 2″ longer than the mouthline. Cut it with warp running lengthwise of strip.

Cut two pieces for pocket linings from silesia or lining fabric, 2″ longer than the length of the mouthline and as deep as is desired for the depth of the pouch of the pocket. The shape of these pieces varies with the slant of the mouthline. The warpline of the pieces is parallel to the warpline of the body of the coat after the pocket is finished. See Figs. 5a, b, c for suggestions for shape and slant of mouthline and for shape and grain of pocket linings.

It is not easy in making a first slot pocket to plan the exact depth of each of the two pieces of pocket lining, since they differ in depth and are treated differently. It is easier to plan and to cut them alike, but 1″ deeper than the planned depth of pocket pouch. When the pocket pouch is formed by joining the two pieces of pocket lining, they may be trimmed to the same size and shape.

Cut a piece of wool fabric to form a facing for the upper edge of the under pocket lining. It may be cut with the same grain and the same shape as this upper edge, but it is only 2″ wide.

CONSTRUCTION

A. *Prepare pocket linings.* Lay a binding strip along the upper edge of upper pocket lining, both with right sides up. Let the binding strip lap over the lining by ⅜". Zigzag over the ⅜" lap, joining wool to lining (Fig. 5d).

 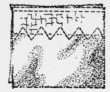

Fig. 5d   Fig. 5e

Lay the piece of wool facing on the upper part of under pocket lining, both with right sides up. Raw edges are matched. Zigzag over the lower raw edge of wool facing and through the pocket lining. Edgestitch the wool and lining together close to the top edge (Fig. 5e).

B. *Attach binding strips.* Pin and baste the stay against the wrong side of the coat, centered on the mouthline.

Lay the wool binding strip, which is attached to the upper pocket lining, along the lower edge of the pocket mouthline, right sides together. Lay the

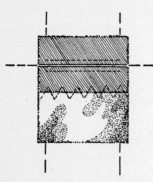

Fig. 5f

other wool binding strip, which is not attached to a piece of pocket lining, along the upper edge of the pocket mouthline. In each case, the binding strip is laid against the right side of the coat and right sides are together (Fig. 5f).

The effect desired in the finished pocket determines the distance between the mouthline and the seamline which is to join the binding strips to the edges of the mouthline.

For a piped effect, the distance between the mouthline and the stitching that joins the binding strip to the mouthline may be as little as ⅛". For a bound effect, it is sometimes ¼". For the effect of pocket lying flush with the surface of the coat, it is often ¼" or more.

Stitch each binding strip to coat on the line as planned and backstitch at each end. The stitching should end exactly on the basting which marks the ends of the pocket mouthline (Fig. 5f).

C. *Cut pocket mouthline.* Cut only fabric of the coat and the stay.

Cut along pocket mouthline, stopping short of each end by ⅜" to ½".

Cut diagonally to each end of each stitching so as to form a triangle of fabric at each end (Fig. 3h).

D. *Press seam edges.* The directions in which the seam edges are to be pressed has been determined by your own choice. Press according to plan.

E. *Turn binding strips to wrong side and finish mouthline.* Turn both binding strips to the wrong side of coat by pulling them through the opening which has been cut.

To finish mouthline when seam edges have been pressed open or when all seam edges have been pressed toward the mouthline: turn the wool strip on each edge of mouthline over the raw edge of seam along mouthline. Fig. 5g shows the treatment along the lower edge of the mouthline. Care should be taken here so that the folded wool strips do not crowd the mouthline opening. The folded edges should exactly meet in order to form two identical narrow rectangles which exactly fill the space between the two stitchings along the mouthline. Baste and press lightly.

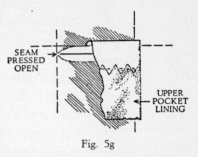

Fig. 5g

To finish mouthline when seam edges have all been pressed away from the mouthline: fold the wool strip so that the folded edge of one exactly meets the folded edge of the other and so that they meet exactly in the center of the opening. Baste and press lightly.

Each of these three finishes now may have a surface stitching which, in each case, is exactly in the groove of the first line of stitching along the mouthline. The ends of stitchings should be securely fastened. Backstitching may be used at the ends, but it should not show as a heavier line of stitching. This surface stitching adds to the durability of the pocket; but it may be omitted.

Overcast the edges of the mouthline together to hold the pocket in its finished position.

Fold coat and pocket stay back until the triangle at each end of mouthline is visible from the wrong side of coat. Backstitch across the base of each triangle. In doing this, be careful that the folded edges meeting along the pocket mouthline continue to meet. The feed dogs of the machine may cause them to separate slightly.

F. *Finish the pocket pouch.* Lay the under pocket lining against the pocket. The wool facing of the pocket lining is against the wrong side of the coat. The upper raw edges of lining with its wool facing should be placed $\frac{1}{4}''$ to $1\frac{1}{2}''$ above the stitching along the edge of mouthline.

Stitch through the lining with its wool facing and through the binding strip of wool and through the stay, but not through the coat, in a line as close as possible to the first stitching along the upper edge of mouthline (Fig. 5h).

Baste and stitch together the loose edges of the pocket linings so as to form a pouch. If their edges do not match, trim them until they do.

G. *Finish the ends of pocket mouthline.* The ends of the mouthline should be finished so as to make them strong and durable. A bar tack may be used, or a line of machine stitching may be placed exactly in the groove at the end, or a fine back-stitching may be put in by hand. If the last is done, the needle should pass straight up and down through the fabrics, as a stabstitch is made. A crow's foot or arrowhead tack, if skilfully executed, is both a strong and a decorative finish.

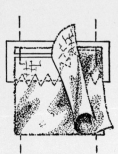

Fig. 5h

H. *Another method for slot pocket with edges piped.* Do not attach the binding strip to the upper pocket lining as suggested above.

Fold each binding strip lengthwise through the middle and right side out. Baste and press.

Lay a folded strip along each edge of mouthline, against the right side of coat. The raw edges are laid toward the mouthline. Each strip is to be stitched to the coat in a line parallel to the mouthline. Each of the two stitchings must be equidistant from the mouthline and equidistant from the folded edge of strips. Stitch each line and back-stitch at each end of mouthline (Fig. 5i).

Fig. 5i

Cut the mouthline as above. The rest of the work is the same as in preceding directions, with one exception, which is: The upper pocket lining is joined to the binding strip along the lower edge of the latter. In doing this, grade the edges of binding strip so that the one next to the coat is longer than the other. Join the shorter edge of binding strip to upper pocket lining with a plain seam pressed open, or by zigzag stitching across lapped raw edges.

REINFORCEMENT OF THE BODY
OF THE COAT

CUTTING

Be sure reinforcement fabric has been thoroughly shrunk and then pressed. The pattern of the coat usually shows how to cut the reinforcement. In general, the back and front are shaped as in Fig. 6.

Fig. 6

The depth along center back line varies from 3″ to as much as 10″. The length along the side seamline is about 3″. The center back may be on warp grainline or on true bias. If it is bias, however, the back should be cut with a seam down the center. The warplines on each half of back should run toward the shoulder and the filling lines toward the underarm. Since a center back

41

seam is not desirable, the center back is usually on warp grain. If the front shoulder of the coat pattern has no shoulder dart, cut the reinforcement in order to provide one. To do so, cut the shoulder seam 1″ longer at each end, at the neck, and at the armscye. This is a total of 2″ added. The coat usually fits and holds its shape better when the reinforcement has a shoulder-to-bust dart.

Cut the back as indicated above.

MARKING

Mark center lines, seamlines, and dartlines with chalk.

CONSTRUCTION

Fitting to the body. Whether you have cut with a dart on the front shoulder, or whether you have cut the shoulder seam 2″ longer than the pattern, follow the procedure below.

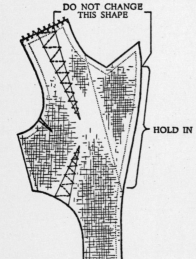

DO NOT CHANGE THIS SHAPE

HOLD IN

Fig. 7

Hold front reinforcement in position on the figure, adjusting it carefully along the bustline.

Slash from center of shoulder to point of bust in straight line.

Lap the cut edges until there is sufficient ease over the bust, and until the filling grain along the bustlines is horizontal. Pin the lapped edges.

Place a short dart 1⅜″ long and ⅜″ wide at the lower front armscye. The line of this dart is from armscye toward bust. It lies under the lower curve of the front armscye of the wool coat where the wool coat is held in (Fig. 7). It is essential to correct fit in this area. Cut, lap edges, and pin as with shoulder dart.

Two other darts in the front may be desirable, although the reinforcement should not be fitted snugly. One dart is in a vertical line from bust to lower edge of reinforcement. The second is on a diagonal line from a point near the bust down toward the side seam. Slash, lap edges, and pin as for shoulder dart.

The back of the reinforcement has darts only if the wool coat has. They are slashed and pinned as are the ones of the front.

Stitching. When all darts have been slashed, lapped, and pinned, zigzag stitch along the raw edges of each dart if the reinforcenment fabric is wigan.

If hymo or similar fabric is used, mark the lines of each dart. Cut on these lines in order to remove a piece of fabric which is of the size and shape of the dart (Fig. 8).

Fig. 8

Bring the raw edges together over a bias strip of wigan which is longer than the dart and about 1″ wide. Stitch through wigan and hymo along each side of dart ⅛″ from the raw edge of hymo. Zigzag stitch up and down dart through both fabrics. This method leaves the dart flat and pliable and easily pressed (Fig. 9).

Shaping. Follow the directions as indicated in Figs. 2 and 7.

Fig. 9

Where directions state "hold in," run a fine gathering thread just outside of the seamline and parallel to it. Draw this thread taut while steaming and pressing.

The ham cushion should be used wherever fabric surface is to be curved. Handle the shaped reinforcement carefully after the shaping is finished, for it may easily lose its curves.

Fit a layer of cotton felt, about 1½″ wide to the front armscye on the inside of the reinforcement, the side next to the body. The felt protects the body from the scratchy hymo. Cut out a ⅜″ dart at the lower section of armscye where there is a similar dart in the reinforcement. Bring the edges together and hold them with overcasting. Let this layer extend to the underarm seam and also 3″ beyond the shoulder seam (Fig. 10). This 3″ extension will be placed across the shoulder seam, and onto the back rein-

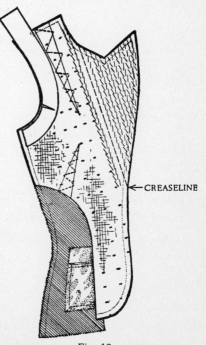

←CREASELINE

Fig. 10

forcement when the shoulder seam is closed. See "Joining Seams of Rein-forcement," page 46. Stabstitch this layer to the reinforcement against the wrong side of the latter.

You will note that there is much shaping to the lower part of the armscye. The wool of the coat front is "held in"; the reinforcement is darted; the layer of felt discussed above is darted; the first layer of shoulder padding is darted. If each of these steps is carefully handled, you will have a good fit at the armscye where fit is essential to the final effect of the finished garment and to retention of shape during the life of the garment.

ATTACHING REINFORCEMENT TO COAT

FRONT

Pockets have been finished and pressed. Darts have been stitched and pressed. Front reinforcement and wool coat front have been shaped separately.

Place front reinforcement on dress form or on body. Place shaped coat front over it, adjusting one to the other along the bustline and pinning.

See that shoulder seams are in place and pin from center of shoulder to bust, then pin from bust downward to lower edge of reinforcement.

While basting the two together, keep them on the dress form. If you have no form, lay them on the table, wool side up, and keep them curved by holding the left hand under them.

Tailor baste from bottom to center shoulder over the fullest part of the bust. Put in four other rows of tailor basting as shown in Fig. 11.

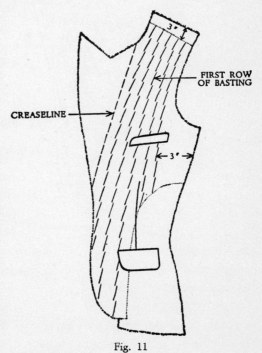

Fig. 11

Note that edges near seamlines are left free for a space of three inches.

Run a fine basting along the creaseline of the lapel, holding the two layers together. All these bastings are left in until the coat is finished and ready for the final pressing.

45

BACK

Place wool over reinforcement, again using a form. Adjust and pin center back lines and shoulders.

Tailor baste center back line and three more lines parallel to it on right and left sides each. Leave edges free near seamlines.

JOINING SEAMS OF REINFORCEMENT

Refer to the outline in "Order of Procedure in Making a Coat," page 20. You will note that many processes are applied to the front of the coat after

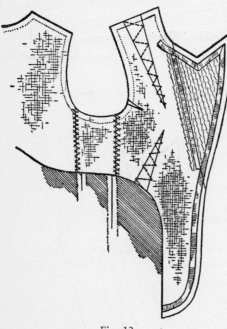

Fig. 12

the first fitting and before joining back and front. Some of the processes are making pockets, padding and taping lapels, basting in reinforcement. Then, after fitting, the shoulder and underarm side seams of the wool are stitched without catching the reinforcement in the seams. The wool seams are pressed open.

To join the shoulder and side seams of the reinforcement, lap the seam edge of the front of the reinforcement over the wool seam. Do not turn under the seam allowance of the reinforcement. Baste together these edges of wool and reinforcement (Fig. 12). It is at this point that the 3" of felt padding, attached to front armscye of reinforcement, is put in position over the back shoulder. This is the extension explained in "Reinforcement of Body of Coat," page 43.

Lap the seam edges of the back of reinforcement over the front along shoulder and underarm seamlines. Pin in place. Catstitch over the raw edge and into the front reinforcement.

Do *not* baste together the seam edges of wool and reinforcement along the armscye line. They are left separate until after the sleeves are stitched into the coat.

LAPEL

Use silk thread matched to wool fabric of coat. Use no knot.

Hold coat in left hand so that lapel rolls *as it is to roll* on the finished coat. This position is not changed throughout the padding of the lapel. Holding the coat in this manner causes the hymo to be pushed up, almost eased onto the wool fabric. The more the hymo is pushed up, the more roll there will be in the finished lapel. For this reason, care should be taken to provide ease where you wish the lapel to roll and to allow little or no ease where the lapel is to lie flat. For the inexperienced worker, it is safe merely to hold lapel over the left hand as suggested above, and not try to push up more or less hymo according to degree of roll desired.

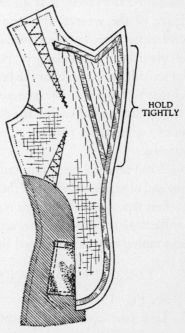

HOLD TIGHTLY

Begin padding ½″ inside of creaseline and parallel to it. Put in a second row inside of the first. ("Inside" means on the side nearer to the bust and away from the outside edge of lapel.) Run these rows up to the neckline seam, but stop them 3″ short of edge of coat at the lower end of creaseline (Figs. 10 and 13).

On the other side of the creaseline, ½″ away from it and parallel to it, place another row of padding. Continue with parallel rows of padding until lapel is fully padded. Pad up to seamlines on lapel, but leave the seam edge free. (Figs. 10 and 13).

Fig. 13

Work along a ridge formed by holding lapel over left hand. Make stitches very small as they go through reinforcement and wool and not more than ½″ long on the reinforcement side. They do not usually show from the wool side, although some tailors allow them to show.

Keep stitches snug but do not allow reinforcement to pucker.

Some tailors begin the padding ¼″ outside of creaseline. This line for beginning the work is equally satisfactory. The directions above may still be followed except that the order of rows of padding is changed.

TAPING THE CREASELINE

Be sure to shrink the tape before using it.

Cut a strip of tape long enough for creaseline plus a 1½″ to 2½″ extension which may later be carried over onto creaseline of collar.

Pin tape on creaseline with one edge on the line and the other away from the lapel and toward the body of the coat. Put tape on tightly.

Pin tape from neckline seam along the creaseline to a point 3″ short of end of creaseline on lapel. Insert pins at right angles to tape. Leave an inch or two of tape hanging free at the lower end.

Hold the coat front up against you to determine how much the creaseline should be shortened, if at all. According to the design of the coat and the figure of the wearer, the tape will be shortened or lengthened and the creaseline, therefore, shortened or lengthened. Also, the tape may need to be shortened in a particular area, perhaps where it crosses the bustline, in order to provide more curve for the bust and to help the front line of the coat to fit closely to the body. The contour of the coat front may be much improved by such adjustment of ease in the coat as it is pinned to the tape. The direction of creaseline is not changed. Only the length of tape and amount of ease are altered.

When tape has been adjusted, cut off the excess at the lower end so that the end of tape is 3″ short of the end of creaseline at edge of lapel (Fig. 13).

Fell tape to reinforcement on each edge, using medium-sized stitches.

Re-mark the edges of lapel according to pattern, if necessary. The padding and taping may have changed the shape slightly.

TAPING THE LAPEL AND FRONT EDGES

See Fig. 13.

Trim coat and reinforcement to ½″ seam allowance along the whole front edge. Trim around lapel to the notch, but do not trim gorgeline.

Press lapel carefully at this time. Check the two sides, right and left, to see that they are identical in size and shape.

Place lapel on table, reinforcement side up. Heavy reinforcements, such as hymo or linen canvas, must be trimmed away exactly on the seamline before the tape is applied. Hymo will not crease and, therefore, it spoils an edge seam that is to be creased. Lightweight reinforcements may be trimmed away along edge of tape after the tape is put on.

The tape along the edge of coat extends from the point where the facing meets the hem at the lower line of coat to a point 1″ beyond the creaseline at the neck (Fig. 13).

Pin outer edge of tape perfectly flat. Allow no fullness in either coat or tape except on lapel as indicated in the next step.

From a point 1″ above the lower end of creaseline to a point 3″ to 4″ from the peak of the lapel, hold the tape tightly. This tightness of tape will help to keep the desired amount of roll in the finished lapel.

Clip or notch the inside edge of the tape where necessary to make it lie flat. The edge of tape that lies on the seamline maintains an unbroken line.

Fell each edge of the tape. First, fell along the seamline. Use thread to match the wool fabric and fell into the wool. The seam edge of hymo reinforcement will have been cut away. The seam edge of wigan will be cut away after this felling is done. Stitches should be exactly on the seamline. Second, fell the other edge of tape to *reinforcement only*, so that stitches do not show from the wool side.

Some tailors prefer to machine stitch on the very edge of the tape and through the wool. As in the method above, the seam edge of the hymo will have been cut away. Only the inside edge of the tape is then felled to the hymo. The machine stitching provides a clean-cut line as a guide to be followed later when the facing is attached.

Wherever tape has been held tight, see that the thread is fastened securely at each end of a tightly held section. Otherwise, the felling may allow the tape to slip up or down slightly and the careful adjustment of tape is lost.

BOUND BUTTONHOLES

MARKING

Be sure center front of coat is marked.

Buttons slide toward the outer end of buttonholes when the coat is being worn. If a thin thread shank is used to sew buttons onto coat, they will slide nearly to the end of buttonholes. Then half of each button lies on the button-hole and most of the other half lies outside the buttonhole toward the edge of the garment. Therefore, the center front of the garment is in a line that lies just inside the outer ends of the buttonholes; the buttonholes are not centered on the center front of the garment. The outer ends of button-holes are far enough away from the edge of garment so that the buttons will not extend over the edge of the gar-ment.

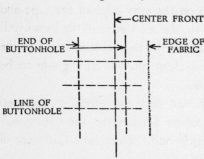

Fig. 14a

Mark the ends of buttonholes by two vertical lines of bastings that run across the ends (Fig. 14a).

Mark the line of each proposed buttonhole with a basting thread on fillingwise grainline of coat fabric. This threadline should extend well beyond the vertical lines that mark the ends. If these lines are not extended, they will be hidden during some of the later work and you will not be able to see where the buttonhole should be placed (Fig. 14a).

PREPARATION OF COAT FOR BUTTONHOLES

This step may be omitted if fine wigan has been used for reinforcement of coat front. It is a necessary process if hymo has been used.

Cut a narrow rectangle, or oval, away from the reinforcement under each line of buttonhole. Over this opening, lay a piece of firm, fine fabric such as fine silesia. Trim so that silesia extends over the opening by ¼" to ½" on all the edges. Catstitch finely to hold silesia to reinforcement (Fig. 14b).

Cutting away reinforcement and putting silesia in place of it are done so that the buttonholes may be made through silesia rather than through stiff, coarse hymo.

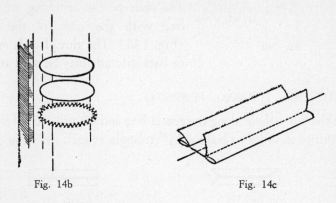

Fig. 14b   Fig. 14c

PREPARING THE TUCKED STRIP

Cut a strip of wool material on the lengthwise or true bias grain. This strip should be about 2" wide and as long as desired. The length depends on the number of buttonholes to be made. Put in a fine marking basting throughout the center. Lay a lengthwise fold ¼" from the center mark with wrong sides of fabric together. Stitch ⅛" from folded edge to form a tuck. If the material is very heavy, the stitching should be a little more than ⅛" from the edge. Fold in a second tuck parallel to the first. The folded edge of the two tucks should be exactly ½" apart. Stitch ⅛" from folded edge as with first tuck. The distance between the two stitchings should be ¼" (Fig. 14c). Extreme accuracy in preparation of this tucked strip is essential. An effective corded result is produced if yarn is pulled through each of these tucks. Use a blunt yarn needle and a yarn that is as coarse as you can run into the tuck.

Cut this tucked strip into lengths. Each length should be 1" longer than the desired length of the buttonhole.

APPLYING TUCKED STRIP

Place a tucked strip on the garment so that:

1. Right side of the tucked piece is against right side of garment.

2. The center marking of the strip is against horizontal marked line of buttonhole.

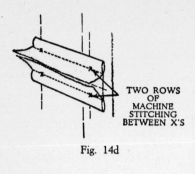

TWO ROWS
OF
MACHINE
STITCHING
BETWEEN X'S

Fig. 14d

3. The tucked strip extends beyond each end of the buttonhole by ½".

Baste this strip into position along its center line. Stitch the strip to the garment on the lines of stitching of the tucks. The ends of the stitching are exactly in line with the ends of the buttonhole (Fig. 14d). The thread ends may be tied, or backstitching may be used at each end.

CUTTING, TURNING, FINISHING

Cut the buttonhole along the center line and then to each of the four ends of stitchings in order to leave a ¼" triangle at each end (Fig. 14e).

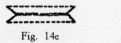

Fig. 14e

Fig. 14f

It is best to do the cutting from the wrong side of the garment. In doing

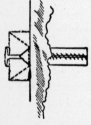

Fig. 14g

so, keep raw edges of tucked strip away from scissors. Cut exactly to the ends of stitching but not beyond.

The ends of the finished buttonhole will be less bulky if you clip the tucked strip from end to end on the center lines. If you do so, note that within the buttonhole, you cut tucked strip and garment; outside of the buttonhole you cut *only* the tucked strip. Be careful not to clip garment when you clip the ends of the tucked strip.

Pull the tucked piece through to the wrong side. Overcast the tucks together so the edges just meet and fill the opening (Fig. 14f). Press lightly from the right side.

Turn the garment to the wrong side and fasten the small triangular pieces with a "U" stitching as shown in Fig. 14g.

Press again.

APPLYING FACING

After the front facing of the coat is attached to the coat, the facing is used to finish the wrong side of the buttonhole by one of the following methods:

Method 1. Cut facing on filling grainline exactly along the line of opening of the buttonhole. Turn edges under against buttonhole so as to form an oval with sharply pointed ends. Fell facing to buttonhole, using extra stitches

at each end to cover the cut edge which cannot be turned under (Fig. 14h).
Method 2. Cut the facing exactly as buttonhole was cut with a triangle

Fig. 14h   Fig. 14i

at each end. Turn under each side and end, and fell facing to buttonhole.
With this method, each of the four corners requires extra stitches to cover
the edge which cannot be turned under (Fig. 14i).

FRONT FACING

Check to see that seam edges of the reinforcement of coat front have been cut away as directed, under "Lapel", page 48.

Place facing to coat, right sides together, coat side up, reinforcement next to the table. Allow facing to extend beyond edge of lapel for about $\frac{1}{4}''$.

Baste the two together, beginning at lower end of creaseline and following creaseline to neckline. Then baste along edge of lapel, following the lapel line but $1''$ to $1\frac{1}{2}''$ from edge. Facing may be held a little tight around curve at bottom of jacket.

Note. Creaseline is often the origin of work and gorgeline is always carefully handled.

Place the coat, facing side up, ease fullness into lapel and baste along seamline. This fullness is eased only from notch at neck to lower end of creaseline. Continue to baste along seamline of lapel for remainder of facing. It is not necessary to baste in fullness from end of creaseline around lower curve of jacket. In fact, facing is held tight.

Stitch lapel with coat side up close to tape, but do not stitch tape. Stitch up to the notch and retrace. Clip seam edge at notch.

Grade the seam edges so that no two edges are the same width. Depending on bulkiness of fabric, the seam edges may be less than $\frac{1}{4}''$ for the narrow one and about $\frac{1}{4}''$ for the wider one. Seam edges that are too wide result in a clumsy edge seam. The longer seam edge should lie against the outside surface of the coat. In lapel, trim coat seam shorter than facing. Below creaseline, trim facing seam shorter than coat.

Press seam open with a light press. Press a small section at a time so as not to alter shape of lapel and coat front. For heavy wool, deaden edge first by dampening, then pressing flat on wood.

Turn facing right side out and shape point with stiletto and fingers. Work edge between fingers so that seam will be rolled slightly to the underside and cannot possibly show from right side. Hold the underside toward you as you work. This will require two bastings, one on lapel

with coat held toward you and one below the lapel creaseline with facing
held toward you. (See Fig. 15 and Glossary, "Rolling Seam to Underside.")

For a hand-finished edge, hand-sew edge with combination backstitch
and running stitch. Use hand-sewing silk (waxed) on a wool coat. Hold
coat as during basting.

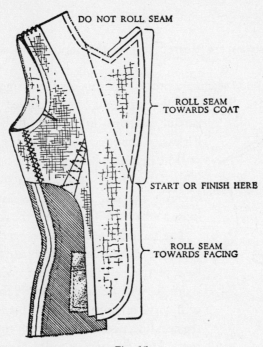

Fig. 15

Hold lapel, rolled as it is to be on the coat, and put in two rows of
tailor basting, the first row through the center of the lapel and the other row
near the creaseline.

Note. Side to be eased is under thumbs in handwork and against feed
dogs in machine work.

SEAMS

In general, seams are treated just as they are in the making of wool dresses.

The vertical body seams are pressed open unless the design of the garment directs otherwise. Several of the seams may be so curved that they need  careful treatment in pressing. If they do not press flat easily, the edges should be clipped so that they will lie perfectly flat against the body of the coat. If the fabric frays easily, it is sometimes wise to overcast the raw edges. Overcasting should be loose so that it will not draw the edge in the least.

The shoulder seam requires treatment different from that in dressmaking. It should be curved at the base of the neckline, so that, when the coat is worn, it will lie smooth across the shoulder and will curve up onto the neck. If it is not curved at the neckline, neither the coat nor the collar will set well. Also, the wearer will feel the weight of the coat hanging from the base of the neck at the

Fig. 16

shoulder. The depth of the curve varies, but slightly less than $\frac{1}{4}''$ is a usual amount (Fig. 16).

According to the style of the period, the rest of the shoulder seam may be a straight, ruled line, or it may be very slightly curved to follow the hollow of the shoulder of the body. The amount of curve here is about $\frac{1}{8}''$.

SHOULDER PADS

For some years shoulder padding has been an important feature in the fashion picture of coats and jackets. A well-fitted pad, correctly made and adjusted to the coat and to the wearer, is a definite help in obtaining a smart effect in the finished garment. A pad which is poorly fitted, made, or adjusted, detracts from the final effect.

Pads for both shoulders should be ready for the first fitting although they may be only semifinished. The final plan for completing them may be worked out during this fitting.

There are several ways to obtain pads. Ready-made ones may be satisfactory, although they usually need some refitting. Pattern companies have published patterns for different types of pads. These may be used although, again, refitting is often necessary. The coat pattern used for the coat usually includes directions for cutting and making pads and they, too, should be fitted to the individual figure and garment. Genuine custom-made pads are designed for the individual figure and for the lines of the coat. They are made according to true tailoring methods, and are correctly adjusted and attached to the coat. They are the ones most satisfactorily used in a custom-made coat. Directions for such pads are presented here.

Two qualities of the finished product are essential. One is graduated edges so that the coat, when worn, lies smooth throughout the shoulder area. A second quality is treatment at the armscye line on the shoulder and at the top of sleeve so that the sleeve falls smoothly. There should be no ridge or line where pads end and no ripple of fabric in top of sleeve due to abrupt ending of shoulder padding.

MATERIALS USED

Cotton felt, sheet wadding of cotton or of wool, and cotton or wool batting are used between layers of unbleached muslin or wigan. A layer of crinoline may be used in place of one of muslin. It makes a stiffer pad, but crinoline tends to soften during wear.

THE BASIC LAYER

Cut one layer of cotton felt, using the pattern of the finished coat front and back as a guide. Cut without seam allowances on shoulder seamline and at underarm seamline. Cut out a ⅜" dart at lower front armscye where there is a dart in the reinforcement. Bring edges of dart together and hold them with an overcasting stitch. Along armscye line, the cutting line depends on the design of shoulder and top of sleeve. For a broad shoulder with a plain, straight-hanging sleeve top, the felt may be cut with the seam allowance provided by the pattern. In that case, leave this seam allowance across the top of the armscye, but trim it off across the underarm curve, be-

tween the notches of the front and back. The seam allowance thus left on the padding provides for the little width needed in addition to the width of the shoulder of the wool coat.

The last line to be determined is a curved one along the inside edge. The degree and shape of curve is based on the needs of the individual figure and the lines of the coat. It provides for three inches of width at the underarm seamline. It usually spans the hollow below the front shoulder, but it does not cover the full-

Fig. 17a   est part of the shoulder blade in the back.

Bring the edges of the shoulder seam, the edges of the underarm seam, and the edges of the dart together and overcast them, so that the edges of each seam or dart meet and lie flat (Fig. 17a).

This layer of padding is the widest and will lie next to the body of the coat. It is now tailor basted to the reinforcement of the coat. The basting may be fine but it should not be drawn tightly.

OTHER LAYERS OF PADDING

These layers are added according to individual needs and according to fashion.

Cut a pattern for each layer from muslin or wigan and then another like it from wadding or batting. The latter gives a bulkier, less solid pad which is

more or less desirable according to the prevailing fashion. Cut these layers without a seam on the shoulder line and do not extend them below the notches on the armscye line; give them the same line across the top of the armscye line as the first layer has (Fig. 17b). Cut each layer narrower than the previous one along the inside

Fig. 17b   Fig. 17c

edges which lie against the body of the coat (Fig. 17c).

Tailor baste muslin and padding together for each layer. In doing so, hold the layers curved just as they will be in the finished coat. Stabstitch each layer to the previous one. In stabstitching layers together, keep the pad in a decided curve over the hand. Tightly drawn stitches will stiffen the pad and pack the layers together. Therefore the pads will not lose shape later when the coat is subjected to hard wear.*

For a coat with rounded shoulders, the muslin pattern for each layer may be seamed along the shoulder seamline so as to give a slight curve over shoulder and top of arm; or the same result may be obtained by one or more short darts from the outer edge toward the shoulder (Figs. 18a and 18b).

Fig. 18a   Fig. 18b

When all layers have been planned and stabstitched together, a final layer of muslin may be laid under the pad to cover the raw edges of the several layers. The muslin may be tailor basted to position. The muslin piece merely protects the raw edges so that they cannot curl or lose their padding during wear or dry cleaning.

STIFFENING OR PADDING FOR TOP OF SLEEVE

If the coat has an exaggeratedly broad shoulder and a plain top sleeve which falls vertically from the armscye line, it may not be necessary to use top-of-sleeve stiffening or padding.

Frequently, however, a slight stiffening or padding is shaped according to the top of the sleeve and attached to the shoulder pad across the top portion of the armscye.

For a slight stiffening, cut a strip of bias from reinforcement fabric and make it 3″ to 4″ wide. Fold it lengthwise through the middle. Stretch the raw edges of this strip onto the shoulder pad across the top of the armscye line. Make it cup slightly as if it were curving over the top of the arm. It serves merely to give a slight body to the top of the wool sleeve and thus prevent the sleeve from forming a ripple at the top.

A slight padding for top of sleeve may be formed of a soft roll of cotton batting covered with soft lining fabric cut on the bias. This roll may be $\frac{1}{2}$″ to 1″ in diameter and 4″ to 5″ long. Attach it to the shoulder pad across the top of the armscye line. It serves the same purpose as the stiffening mentioned above, and is slightly preferable for a coat with average width of shoulder and a well-curved top of sleeve.

* If the shoulder bone is prominent, as it often is with thin persons, pull out some of the padding to make a slight hollow where the shoulder bone will fit into the pad.

The finished pad is attached to the reinforcement of the coat near each end of the shoulder seam and at front and back of armscye. Short, swing tacks are used, so that the pad is securely but not rigidly fastened to the coat.

The other loose edges of the pad may be attached in three or four places, again firmly but not rigidly.

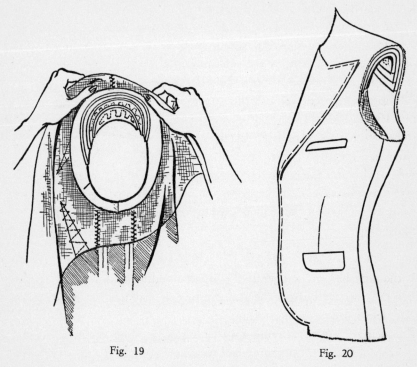

Fig. 19   Fig. 20

Around the underarm curve of the armscye line, a stabstitch may be used to attach the basic layer of felt to the reinforcement and felt which have already been placed in the body of the coat.

Fig. 19 shows the basic layer and the several layers with graduated edges, as they appear from the inside of the coat. Fig. 20 shows them from the outside of the coat before the sleeve is inserted.

UNDERCOLLAR

The value of correct methods and of accurate work in the preparation of the undercollar cannot be overemphasized. If the set of collar and shoulders is good, it gives style to the entire coat. Tailors are proud of their patterns for undercollars. It is a mark of esteem when a tailor gives another person his prized collar pattern.

CUTTING

Cut with ½" seam allowance on each edge.

Since there is to be a center back seam, cut two pieces of linen canvas and two pieces of undercollar fabric. The latter may be melton or coat fabric. The canvas must be fully shrunk and thoroughly pressed.

Cut both melton and canvas with center back seams with the usual ½" seam allowance. Cut with each center back on a true bias so that each *gorgeline* is on a true *warpline*. In this way the right and left halves of canvas collar and of wool undercollar will have identical grainlines and therefore will have the same degree of stretch on right and left sections (Fig. 21a).

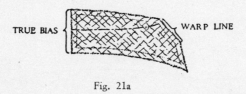

Fig. 21a

When one side of a collar does not fit to the neck as snugly as does the other side, or when one end of the collar does not lie flat, the reason may be that the right and left sides were not cut as directed above.

MARKING

Chalkmark the full length of the creaseline on each piece. At center back, the fall must be deeper than the stand.

Chalkmark all seamlines.

CONSTRUCTION

Measure the exact size of finished neckline of coat from the center back to the front end of gorgeline, where collar and lapel will form the notch. This measurement determines location of center back seam of the collar. Take measurements of neckline and of collar on the stitching lines of seams, not on the cut edges.

Join the two undercollar pieces of canvas and the two of wool to conform to these measurements, making center back seams wider or narrower as needed. Lap the raw edges of the canvas without turning back an edge of either piece. Machine stitch through the two pieces so that the stitching is exactly in the center back.

Make a plain seam in the wool undercollar, with the machine stitching exactly in center back. Press seam edges open. Press on wood to make the seam very flat.

Place wool undercollar on top of canvas reinforcement with wrong side of wool against canvas. Lay flat on table and baste together along creaseline (Fig. 21b). Stitch along the creaseline just up to the seamline at each end, but not to the raw edge. Retrace the stitching at each end. Hold canvas toward you, and pad the stand in vertical rows between creaseline and neckline. Start along center back. Pad only up to the marked seamlines (Fig. 21b). The stand is sometimes machine stitched lengthwise of collar stand, instead of padstitched.

Hold the collar curved over the left hand as you pad the fall in horizontal rows. Start at center back and keep rows parallel to outer edge of the fall. Leave $\frac{1}{2}''$ seam allowances without padding (Fig. 21b).

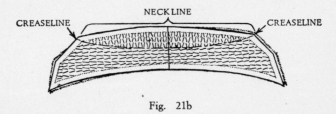

Fig. 21b

PRESSING AND SHAPING

There is much difference of opinion as to the best method for this process. Two methods are suggested here. The first is the simpler and it allows less possibility of error in the hands of a beginner. It is one used by many custom tailors.

Method 1. Lay collar on wood, with the canvas side up. Moisten and press the stand and the fall separately, pressing each only up to the creaseline. Be careful not to stretch any part, for it is easy to stretch an edge without realizing you have done so. Fold collar on creaseline. Lay it on board with the fall side down and press again (Fig. 21c).

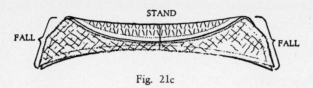

Fig. 21c

Open the collar, but do not attempt to lay it flat except as directed here. Press flat only ½″ at each end of the creaseline, the ½″ that lies between the raw edge and the stitching line of the seam. This edge is pressed flat in order to simplify a later process.

Method 2. On wood, with canvas side up, moisten and press the stand and the fall separately. Then fold on creaseline and press with fall side down.

Again on wood, lay collar open with canvas side up, but do not lay collar flat because the creaseline is to remain pressed into a fold. Stretch and press the stand and the fall separately. The pressing iron will form a slight circular motion as you press each section. In this way, the neckline and the outer edge of the collar are slightly stretched and the creaseline is slightly shrunk. Work carefully so as to keep fall and stand smoothly pressed. There should be no rippled edges such as result from overstretching an outer edge.

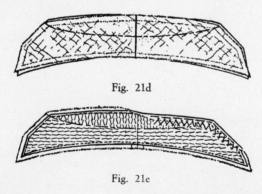

Fig. 21d

Fig. 21e

Fold on creaseline. Press only the creaseline, keeping the stand side up. Press until dry.

Open collar. Press flat the ½″ at each end of creaseline between the raw edge and seamline.

By this method the inexperienced worker may overstretch the edges, so that it is wise to recheck the length of the neckline of the collar. If it is more than ½″ to ¾″ longer than it was before pressing and shaping, it is overstretched. Re-pressing will usually correct the error. If it does not, the seam in the center back of collar should be taken deeper, or the front ends of collar recut. Neither of these corrections is easy to make or desirable. It is far easier to avoid overstretching during the first shaping and pressing.

ATTACHING UNDERCOLLAR TO COAT

PRESSING CREASELINE ON THE BODY OF THE COAT

Lay the front facing of the coat out of the way. Fold the creaseline in the lapel of the coat and reinforcement exactly on the line planned for it. Press this creaseline close to the neckline and for one inch down from the neckline. The rest of the length of the creaseline is not pressed. Do not press any creaseline in the front facing.

Following these directions results in pressing a crease along the creaseline for one inch only and in body of coat and reinforcement only. The lapel will fold back along the creaseline when the coat is finished, even though the fold is not pressed into a crease. The one-inch pressed crease and the taping and padding of lapel help it to do so.

RETESTING FIT AND DESIGN OF UNDERCOLLAR

Fit and pin the undercollar to the neckline with raw edges lapped so that seamlines coincide. Match center back lines of coat and of collar, also creaselines of coat and collar. Hold collar taut across the back and hold collar easy across the shoulder. There is not enough ease to affect the length of collar, but there is enough to make collar set well and to give comfort to the wearer (Fig. 22).

Adjust collar between creaseline and notch, if necessary. This adjustment affects the roll of the lapel, the roll of the collar, and the width across end of collar. It is important. Try on form to test fitting. Place pins perpendicular to seamline across the back and up to the fold of creaseline. In adjusting gorge-line, lap raw edges of coat and collar and place pins

Fig. 22

in line with seamline (Fig. 22). Watch to see that center back of fall coincides with center back of coat. Chalkmark seamlines on collar and coat.

TREATMENT FOR UNDERCOLLAR OF MELTON

After fitting collar to neckline, remove collar from coat. Cut away seam allowances on neckline and gorgeline of undercollar. Seam allowances are left on neckline and gorgeline of coat. Stitch the edge of the stand and of the gorgeline with the wool side up. The stitching lies ⅛″ from edge and so is inside the seamline. Trim the canvas close to the stitching, but leave the melton edge ⅛″ wide. Note that this trimming occurs only on edge of stand and gorgeline. Pin collar in place again. Baste with lapped raw edges, from center back to notch on each side.

Working from right to left, fell to coat from notch to notch, beginning at the lapel-collar notch on the right-hand side of the coat. Use waxed hand-sewing silk. For method of waxing, see "Prepare buttonhole twist", page 92. Do not catch facing of lapel. You may catch reinforcement. Surface stitches should be perpendicular to raw edge and close together. Hold collar in left hand as you work.

On the wrong side of neckline, trim coat and reinforcement to ½″ and ¾″ seam, respectively. Catstitch the longer edge, which is the reinforcement, firmly to the canvas stand of undercollar. Clip where necessary to make the seam edge lie flat (Figs. 23a and 23b). Use dress form to test results, or try it on.

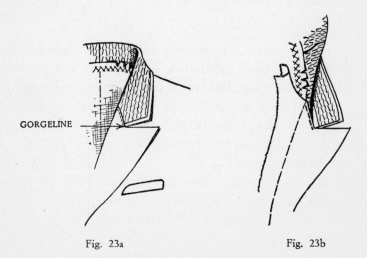

GORGELINE

Fig. 23a   Fig. 23b

The inch or more of tape that was left loose at upper end of lapel crease-line may now be carried onto the collar along its creaseline. It should be held snug.

Put coat on the form and retest the shape of ends of collar in relation to peak of lapel. Leave no seam allowance on collar ends. The depth of the fall at center back and the width of the end of collar often measure the same.

Stitch ends and fall of collar $\frac{1}{4}''$ to $\frac{3}{8}''$ from raw edge. Bulky fabrics may need $\frac{3}{8}''$. Do not trim canvas away, but trim canvas and wool to an even width.

TREATMENT FOR UNDERCOLLAR OF COAT FABRIC

If coat fabric is firm and does not fray, it may be treated exactly as if melton were used.

For fabrics that fray, fit collar to coat, retesting the neckline, gorgeline, and ends. Stitch all around the collar, stand and fall $\frac{1}{4}''$ to $\frac{3}{8}''$ from edge (Fig. 21d). Trim canvas close to stitching, but leave the seam allowance on the wool.

Turn raw edge of wool over the linen canvas all around the edge, stand, and fall. Turn corners carefully so as to retain original shape. Baste and press lightly.

Catstitch over raw edge of wool and into linen canvas. Press firmly (Fig. 21e, page 63).

Pin collar in place. Baste.

Follow directions above for melton in order to fell undercollar to coat along neckline and gorgeline, and to finish neckline seam on the wrong side. The rest of the directions for melton may be disregarded because the ends and fall of collar have already been tested and edges finished.

LOCATING GORGELINE OF FRONT FACING

Put coat on form to determine the gorgeline on the wool facing of front of coat. It may not exactly follow the gorgeline of the undercollar, but it must start at the notch and form part of a trim line from the peak of the lapel to the neckline.

Turn in the front facing along the gorgeline and baste the turned edge, but do not baste it to the coat (Figs. 23a and 23b). Trim away any extra material on facing or clip seam edge, if necessary, to make it lie flat.

TOPCOLLAR

CUTTING

The center back of topcollar is on warpwise grain. Use strip of fabric at least 2″ longer than undercollar and at least 1″ wider.

MARKING

Mark center back with basting.

Use undercollar pattern to chalkmark the creaseline onto the topcollar fabric. Mark this line with basting. Allow ½″ seam at the neckline edge. Chalkmark all seamlines along edges.

SHAPING

The topcollar is shaped according to the method used for shaping the undercollar. Methods 1 and 2 below refer to corresponding numbers for method used with undercollar.

Method 1. Lay the collar, right side of fabric down, against wood. Press the stand and the fall separately, only up to the creaseline in each case. This pressing is light and it does no shaping of the collar.

Fold the collar along the creaseline. The creaseline is not pressed, but from this point on, the topcollar is kept folded along the creaseline. Whenever it is laid down, it is kept folded. If handled carefully, the collar will tend increasingly to hold its own creaseline. The peculiar qualities of wool fabric help it to do so.

Method 2. Lay the collar, right side of fabric down, against wood. Press the stand and the fall separately, only up to the creaseline in each case. This first pressing is a light one and it does no shaping of collar.

Now press the stand up to the creaseline, using a slight circular motion of iron, as you did on the undercollar when shaping it. Keep the iron well up onto the collar and nearly to the creaseline. The circular motion will tend to stretch the neckline edge; keeping the iron nearly up to creaseline will tend to prevent overstretching. It is easy to overstretch, and it is easy to stretch the portion close to the edge so that the edge ripples. The latter does not result if the edge of the iron is kept close to the creaseline.

Press the fall of collar in the same manner.

While you are shaping the stand and fall separately, you are also tending to shrink the creaseline, even though you are not consciously trying to do so. This slight shrinkage of creaseline is desirable.

Fold the collar along the creaseline and check carefully to see if edges are overstretched and rippled. If they are, re-pressing can correct the difficulty.

ATTACHING TOPCOLLAR TO UNDERCOLLAR OF MELTON

Place the topcollar on the undercollar, matching center back and crease-line. Keep the fold on the creaseline.

Hold the collar folded on the creaseline and tailor baste near the crease-line and parallel to it along the stand.
Repeat on the fall side, near to, but not on, the creaseline. Keep the topcollar easy, not taut, between these two lines of tailor bastings (Fig. 24a). This ease in topcollar allows the collar to remain folded along the creaseline as planned.

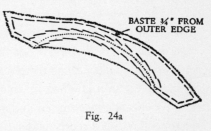

BASTE ¼" FROM OUTER EDGE

Fig. 24a

Baste ¾" from the outer edges, starting at center back and working toward the end on each side (Fig. 24a).

The topcollar requires extra length and width near each end in order to lie flat when finished. The extra size will be provided by allowing ease between this last line of basting and the edge of the collar as indicated in the next step.

Trim the seam allowance of topcollar to ⅜" or ½" beyond the edge of undercollar. Turn edge of topcollar over so that it is placed between the wool undercollar and the canvas reinforcement (Fig. 24b). In basting this turned edge, keep the topcollar eased as mentioned above. The degree of ease varies with the thickness and firmness of fabric, but you should be able to see actual ease between the first
basting near the outer edge and the
turned edge. Some extra trimming
may have to be done to prevent
crowding, for the turned edge of
the topcollar should lie smooth

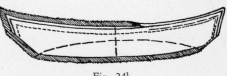

Fig. 24b

and flat between the wool and canvas of undercollar. Since the canvas and wool undercollar have been trimmed to identical size, you will find that the folded edge of the topcollar extends slightly beyond the edge of the wool undercollar (Fig. 24b). Note that the cut edge of the melton is not turned back or under in any way. The fabric is firm and nonfraying, therefore the edge does not need to be turned under. Watch grainlines at end of collar. Miter the wool around the corners in order to retain the original shape and to eliminate bulk.

ATTACHING TOPCOLLAR TO UNDERCOLLAR OF COAT FABRIC

Directions above may be followed except in turning under the outer edge of topcollar. With this type of undercollar, you have a folded outer edge instead of two cut edges. Therefore, turn under the edge of topcollar so that its folded edge extends slightly beyond the edge of undercollar, and all raw edges lie between the two collars. Be especially careful to leave the needed ease in the fabric of the topcollar. Turn the corners carefully so as to retain the original shape of collar. It may be necessary to miter the corners to decrease bulk.

It is slightly more difficult to keep a smooth flat surface of topcollar by this method than it is when melton is used. There are two reasons: there are two wool seam edges turned under instead of one; the two edges of under- and topcollars lie directly under the surface of the topcollar instead of one edge lying between the linen canvas and the undercollar.

FINISHING THE GORGELINE

Turn under the seam edge of gorgeline of topcollar so as to meet the gorgeline of coat facing which has already been turned under and basted (Fig. 25).

Avoid removing ease in topcollar. Trim seam allowance, if necessary. This folded edge should exactly meet the folded edge of the facing. Slipstitch finely and firmly, joining the gorgelines of facing and collar as in Fig. 25. Use thread that matches wool fabric. If these edges are correctly turned under and if slipstitching is as fine and firm as it should be, the gorgeline will be flat and smooth and the stitches completely buried in the fabric.

FINISHING NECKLINE OF FACING AND TOP COLLAR

Treat just as for gorgeline. In fact, the neckline seam here is a continuation of the gorgeline seam.

Fig. 25

FINISHING NECKLINE OF TOPCOLLAR ACROSS THE BACK

In a lined coat, the topcollar may extend onto the coat and be covered by the lining. In this case, clip seam edge of topcollar at a point ½″ forward of the upper end of front facing. This point lies forward of the shoulder seam and under the facing, for the neckline of front facing and collar has been slipstitched (Fig. 26). By clipping, the seam edge of topcollar and facing may lie open and flat through neckline and gorgeline, but the seam allowance of collar across the back of neckline may be turned down onto the coat.

Fig. 26

Catstitch the raw edge of topcollar to the reinforcement of the coat (Fig. 26). These stitches are taken through the reinforcement but not through the wool fabric of the body of the coat. Keep collar folded along the creaseline so that the shape of collar will be retained, and the topcollar will still lie easily over the undercollar.

Another finish across the back neckline of a lined coat consists of a facing of coat fabric. This facing is fitted to the coat across the back and is the same width as the end of the front facing where the facing is cut off at the shoulder line. The shoulder seamline between front facing and back facing is stitched in a plain seam and pressed open. Each of the two edges may be turned under so that the folded edges just meet. Then the edges may be slipstitched together.

This wool facing across the back of neck is joined to the topcollar by a plain seam along the neckline. The seam is pressed open. It is unnecessary to clip the seam edge of collar because all seam edges lie open. This is the same method as that for unlined jackets (Fig. 87).

The lower raw edge of the facing across back may be left raw and will later be covered by the coat lining. The raw edge is sometimes turned under and stitched near the edge. If that is done, the lining is slipped under this finished edge. This latter finish is bulkier and stiffer than the first and may show as a ridge from the right side of the finished coat.

FINISHING OUTER EDGE OF TOPCOLLAR

Fell the undercollar and the topcollar together around the outer edge. Begin work at the lapel-collar notch on the right-hand side of the coat. Hold the bulk of the coat toward you, the collar away from you.

Hold the collar in the left hand. Point the needle toward the stand as you sew, and take small close-set stitches. Draw thread taut. Keep collar folded along the creaseline.

If melton has been used for the undercollar, the felling stitches in this process pass over the cut edge of melton and into the fabric of the topcollar. If coat fabric has been used, they pass over the folded edge of undercollar and into the fabric of the topcollar. In neither case do they catch into the outside layer of the topcollar and therefore they do not show from the right side.

FIRST FITTING OF SLEEVE

Plain Sleeve Without Darts or Gathers

These directions are for a first fitting of sleeve when the coat was fitted without sleeves basted into position.

MARKING

Warp lines and filling lines in the cap of the sleeve should have been marked with basting threads.

The elbow line should be marked. If there is an elbow dart, this is sufficient; if not put in a basting line.

There may be two or three lines of fine gathering threads around the top of cap between the two sets of notches. With three lines, one lies on seamline; one about $\frac{1}{8}''$ inside; and one about $\frac{1}{8}''$ outside of seamline. If there are two lines of gathering threads around the top of the cap, one of these lines is on the proposed line of stitching for the seam. The other line is about $\frac{1}{8}''$ outside of the first line; that is, it is on the seam allowance, nearer the cut edge than is the first thread.

Be sure that the armscye line on the body of the coat has been established and carefully marked.

Close the front opening of the coat and pin as if the coat were buttoned.

BASTING

The lengthwise seams of the sleeve are basted.

The lower edge of the sleeve is turned up and basted on the line suggested by the pattern.

PINNING INTO PLACE DURING FIRST FITTING

Slip the basted sleeve over the arm and bring the underarm curve up to the under part of the arm. Do not stretch the sleeve in doing so.

Drop the arm into its natural position.

Check position of the marking line at elbow. Raise or lower sleeve, if necessary.

Watching to see that the warp lines and filling lines in the sleeve cap are, respectively, vertical and horizontal, adjust the topmost part of the curve of sleeve cap against the coat. The seam allowance on the sleeve cap may or may not be turned under at this time. It is easier to handle the fitting procedures, if the edge is left flat, not turned under (Fig. 27).

See that the stitching line of the seam around the sleeve cap and the corresponding line of the armscye of the coat are exactly matched.

The pattern marking at the top of the sleeve cap, which indicates where the sleeve should meet the shoulder seam of the coat, may not be in the best position. It often needs to be brought forward by $\frac{1}{4}''$ to $\frac{1}{2}''$. Whether or not this change is made, the basted warpline of sleeve cap should be vertical.

Now readjust the basted filling line of sleeve cap so that it is truly horizontal. At the place of the notches in the sleeve cap, adjust the sleeve to the coat. Make the seam stitching line of the sleeve cap meet the seam stitching line of the armscye of the coat. Pin sleeve to coat at the notches, first on the front side of the sleeve and then on the back side.

Fig. 27

Gently draw up the two or three gathering threads in the sleeve cap seamline. They should not be drawn too tightly. Ease the fabric along these threads, adjusting the gathers with three things in mind: the filling grainlines remain horizontal; two or three inches across the topmost part of the curve of cap have very little or no ease; the ease is placed between the end of the plain section just mentioned and the notches of the sleeve on the front side of the sleeve and also on the back. Distribute the ease as uniformly as possible and pin the sleeve to the coat. Place all pins in this fitting at right angles to the armscye seamline. Do not try, at this time, to pin the underarm curve of the sleeve into the coat.

When the first fitting of both sleeve and coat is finished, mark with fine bastings crosswise of the armscye seamline and onto coat and sleeve so as to show where sleeve fits into coat. Such marks should be at each end of the eased portions of cap in back and in front and at top of cap where the shoulder seamline meets the sleeve (Fig. 29).

Turn the coat in order to hold the wrong side of the coat toward you and let the underarm curve of the sleeve fall against the coat along the armscye line. If the seam edges or stitching lines of seam on coat and sleeve do not coincide, do not try to force them to meet. The sleeve should not be stretched along the underarm curve. The coat will not stretch along this line, for it has been taped to prevent stretching. Holding sleeve under thumbs, pin sleeve into position against coat.

Baste across the seamline of sleeve and coat in two or three places, as you did on the upper part of sleeve.

TEST OF FITTED SLEEVE

A well-fitted sleeve may be recognized by the following:

Warplines fall from top of sleeve downward. Filling lines lie in horizontal lines (Fig. 28).

From a direct front and direct back view, the outside or silhouette lines fall vertically.

From a direct side view, the two outside lines of each sleeve fall vertically.

The sleeve is enough larger than the arm to allow for two slight, soft folds of fabric which fall in vertical lines, one from the front and one from the back of the armscye line. These two folds are easily seen either from a direct side view or a straight front view.

Fig. 28

SLEEVES

CUTTING

Wool sleeves were cut when rest of coat was cut.

MARKING

Thread-mark or chalkmark seamlines, hemline, folded edges of vent, button and buttonhole positions. Baste line of warp and filling in top part of cap of sleeve.

Fig. 29

BASTING INTO ARMSCYE LINE OF COAT

Whenever sleeves are basted into armscye line of coat, it is better and easier to baste left sleeve first. Begin work at front seam of two-piece sleeve or at front notches of a one-piece sleeve. Baste across top of cap. Hold the sleeve side under the thumb. Then continue the basting around the lower, underarm curve.

By following these directions, you see readily how to adjust ease in sleeve cap. When you baste in the other sleeve you know where and how ease should be adjusted, even though your work must begin at the back seam of sleeve or at the notches in the back. The right sleeve also is held under the thumbs during the basting.

SHAPING OF CAP

These directions supplement those under "Pressing," page 110.

After sleeves are fitted, either in first or second fitting, baste *across* armscye seamline and onto coat and sleeve in five or six places so as to show how sleeve is related to armscye of coat (Fig. 29). Secure gathering threads

in sleeve cap between each two of these marking lines, so that gathers cannot shift after sleeve is ripped out. If three rows of gathering threads are
used, the center one is on the seamline. The other two are $\frac{1}{8}''$ to each side
of the center one. Be sure seamlines of sleeve cap and of armscye line of coat
are carefully marked with a basting line. Remove sleeve from coat. Rip open
back (elbow) sleeve seam, or the one seam of a one-piece sleeve. Shrink out
fullness in sleeve cap by steaming it over a ham cushion (Fig. 30). If

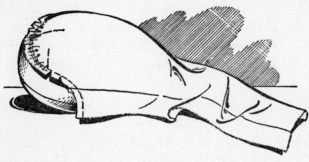

Fig. 30

gathering threads tend to leave marks on wool, remove as soon as possible
the *one* thread that shows inside of the sleeve on seamline, when three
threads are used. Inside the seamline, there should remain no evidence of
gathers or shrinking. Outside the seamline there may be slight gathers and
even tiny darts left visible.

Instead of three gathering threads as suggested above, you may find it
more satisfactory to use only two. If so, one is placed exactly on the line of
stitching of the seam, and the other one is placed $\frac{1}{8}''$ outside of the stitching
line toward the raw edge. With the two threads only, there is no danger of
leaving pressing marks from the thread on the body of the sleeve.

Machine stitching may be used for gathering threads. Since it does not
slip so easily as hand-run gathering threads, machine threads do not need to
be fastened to hold gathered portions of sleeve in place. However, the
sleeve should be handled carefully when it is ripped out and shaped, for the
gathers can slip even along machine stitched gathering threads. If machine
stitching is used, the stitch is of medium length and the tension is slightly
loose, just loose enough so that the fabric can be made to slip along
the thread. If the tension is too loose, the fabric will slip along the thread
when you do not wish it to do so.

After sleeve cap is shaped and while the wool fabric is still slightly
moist, hang sleeve over a soft pad until the wool has thoroughly dried.

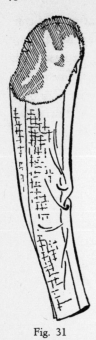

Fig. 31

The shoulder pad, pinned to a dress hanger, may be a sat-isfactory pad for this purpose. As the wool dries, the sleeve cap takes the form of curve desired.

STRETCHING OF SLEEVE SEAM

The front edge of the front sleeve seam may be stretched about ½″ along the line of the inside curve of the arm. If the sleeve has only one part and, therefore, only one seam, the front edge of the one seam may be stretched. Stretching along this line tends to reduce the crosswise wrinkles in the sleeve (Fig. 31). Some tailors not only never use this idea, but are opposed to the technique of stretching wool.

CONSTRUCTION OF TAILORED, TWO-PIECE SLEEVE WITH VENT

When seams are basted and sleeve is laid flat on table with under section up, the seams lie as follows: Front seam follows the general line of the foldline and about ¾″ inside of foldline at the wrist. Back or elbow seam lies just inside the fold from the wristline to a point about 6″ above wristline. From that point on up to the armscye line, it slants toward the under-section so that it does not show when coat is being worn (Fig. 31). An exception to this loca-tion of line is when the sleeve has been designed according to a man's coat sleeve.

Upper section of vent laps over undersection. Length of opening varies. It is about 2½″ for two buttons, 3¼″ to 4″ for three buttons.

A. *Stitch and press open the front sleeve seam.*

B. *Cut reinforcement.* Reinforcement may be bias or fitted. It is usually bias when the lower area of sleeve is of standard design, either with or without a vent. If fitted, cut it with the warpwise grain following the closed front sleeve seam.

Cut ½″ wider than the length of vent.

Allow ¼″ seam on lower edge and on the overlap (top section) edge of vent.

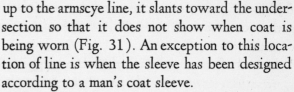

Fig. 32

On the underlap edge of vent, cut exactly like the sleeve (Fig. 32).

C. *Place reinforcement.* Place reinforcement in sleeve so that ¼" extends below the foldline of hem and ¼" beyond the foldline of overlap of vent (Fig. 32). Tailor baste from the wool side. As with the reinforcement in hem of coat, the edge of bias strip may just meet the foldline of the hem, if you wish.

Working from reinforcement side and using thread to match wool, make a long and short basting stitch on foldlines of hem and on overlap of vent and along seamline of underlap, so that thread does not show from the right side. This basting remains in finished coat (Fig.-32).

D. *Make bound buttonholes.* Do not face them until after the vent is finished.

E. *Finish vent and hem.*

OVERLAP. Turn hem, then the overlap of vent. Fold lower edge of overlap (a slight mitering), so that it will not show at the line of hem (Fig. 33). Or miter the corner by use of a stitched seamline as follows: With foldline of hem and vent laid in, mark position of a seam that will run from the outer corner formed by the two foldlines to the corner formed by two raw edges of hem and vent. Turn wrong side out and stitch along marked seamline. Trim, lay seam open, and press. Properly done, this process leaves the end of seam at the outer corner with a folded, but uncut edge.

UNDERLAP. Turn ¼" edge of wool and of reinforcement of the underlap back onto reinforcement and catstitch both raw edges to reinforcement. Turn under, in a diagonal line, the corner of wool that extends onto the area of the lower hem of sleeve (Fig. 33).

Press hem and vent on wood, wool side down.

Catstitch sleeve hem and overlap of vent to reinforcement with long, loose stitches (Fig. 33). Catch top edge of reinforcement to wool of sleeve with long, very loose stitches, like basting. Thread used matches the wool; stitches remain in coat.

F. *Finish bound buttonholes.*

G. *Make worked buttonholes before elbow seam is closed.* These are usually imitation buttonholes. See directions under "False buttonholes," page 95.

H. *Close elbow seam.* Cut diagonally from edge of seam to the upper end of vent-opening on the overlap. (Fig. 34). Baste and stitch elbow seam. Clip the seam edge of the undersleeve at the top of the vent so that underlap may be pressed toward the upper sleeve even though the sleeve seam will be pressed open.

Press elbow seam.

Place laps of vent in correct position. On the wrong side, catstitch raw edges of clipped seams together at the upper end of vent (Fig. 35). Fig. 36 shows right side of finished sleeve.

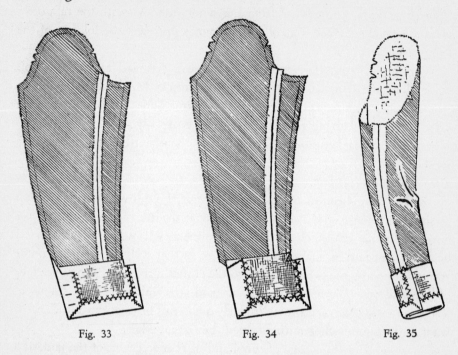

Fig. 33　　　　　　　　　Fig. 34　　　　　　　　　Fig. 35

CONSTRUCTION OF TWO-PIECE SLEEVE WITHOUT VENT

Seamlines lie in the same position as for two-piece sleeve with vent.

A. *Stitch and press front seam and elbow seam.*

B. *Cut reinforcement.* Use bias or fitted piece as for sleeve with vent. Cut 2½″ to 3″ wide.

C. *Place reinforcement.* Place reinforcement in sleeve so that ¼″ extends below the foldline of wool hem (Fig. 37b).

Lap raw edges of reinforcement along the line of elbow seam and cat-stitch edges together (Fig. 37b). Tailor baste from the wool side.

Working from reinforcement side, and using thread to match wool, make a long and short basting stitch along foldline of hem, catching reinforcement to wool. This basting remains in finished coat and so should not show from right side (Fig. 37b).

D. *Finish hem.* Turn wool hem over reinforcement. Baste and press lightly.*

* Catstitch the raw edge of wool hem to the reinforcement. Catstitch the upper edge of reinforcement to the free edges of seams of wool sleeve (Fig. 37a).

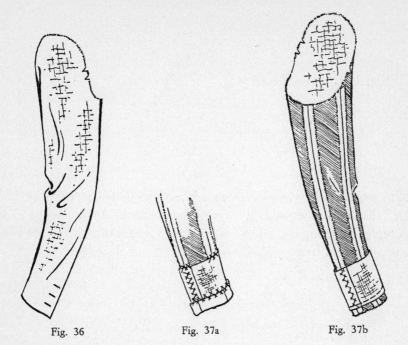

Fig. 36   Fig. 37a   Fig. 37b

CONSTRUCTION OF ONE-PIECE SLEEVE

This is the same as for the two-piece sleeve without vent; the only difference in treatment is that shaping is done with no seam stitching.

SLEEVE LININGS

CUTTING

Cut exactly as wool sleeves except cut the underarm curve of lining higher than the corresponding curve of wool sleeve. At the lowest part of this curve, the lining is cut 1½″ higher. The curve is then graduated so that the upper half of lining and of wool sleeve are cut alike (Fig. 38).

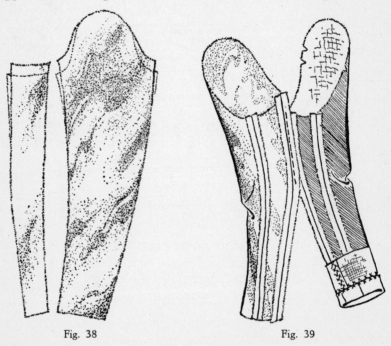

Fig. 38   Fig. 39

MARKING

Mark seam allowances and notches according to sleeve pattern.

CONSTRUCTION FOR TWO-PIECE SLEEVE WITH VENT

Stitch seams and press open.
Turn both wool and lining sleeves wrong side out.

Baste lining to wool sleeve so that elbow seam of lining is caught to elbow seam of wool. In doing this, use a heavy thread and a long and short basting stitch, catching together only the free seam edges. Leave unbasted 3" at top and bottom of seamline. Keep lining slack though not actually eased (Fig. 39).

Turn so that wool sleeve lies inside of lining sleeve and lining is right side out. Baste lining and sleeve together above the vent.

Turn under the lower edges of lining and place them against wool hem and vent so that 1" or more of wool shows above foldline of hem and inside of vertical foldline of vent on the upper lap. The lining of underlap of vent is placed ⅛" to ¼" inside of the foldline of the wool.

Fell lining to sleeve along both edges of vent and along hemline.

Note that seam edges of lining have to be clipped on the diagonal so as to form right angles around upper end of vent.

CONSTRUCTION FOR TWO-PIECE SLEEVE WITHOUT VENT OR FOR ONE-PIECE SLEEVE

Close seams and press open.

Turn wool and lining sleeves wrong side out and catch seam edges together as above (Fig. 39).

Turn so that wool sleeve lies inside of lining sleeve and lining is right side out.

Finish lower edge of lining. Turn raw edge of lining under ½" so that lining laps over wool hem at least ½". Pin and baste ⅜" from this folded edge. If all precautions have been observed, the lining is somewhat longer than the wool sleeve. The extra length lies as a slight fold near the top of the wool hem. The part of the wool hem which shows below the lining is about 1".

Turn back the folded edge of lining ¼" and fell one thickness of lining to the wool hem. (Fig 40) This leaves a tucklike fold with no felling showing.

Baste with long and short stitches so as to hold lining to the reinforcement along the upper edge of reinforcement (Fig. 40). The extra length of lining due to the lining having been held slack now lies above this basting line. Since this basting remains in sleeve, it should be of matching thread and should be invisible from the right side.

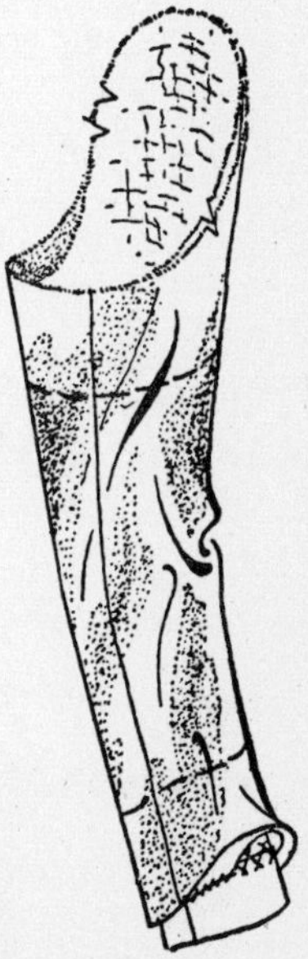

Fig. 40

TREATMENT OF UPPER SLEEVE

Baste lining to sleeve along a filling line that lies 3″ to 4″ below lowest curve of armscye line (Fig. 40). The lining seems loose and full, but do not cut off any length until you find it necessary when adjusting lining of sleeve and coat.

At this time, sleeve is stitched into coat.

REPLACING SLEEVE IN COAT

Pin and baste sleeve into its former position relative to coat. Be sure to match each pair of markings on armscye lines of coat and of sleeve. Also, see that the ease that was held in at lower front and lower back armscye of coat is still held in.

When basting sleeves into position, somewhat better results are obtained if the left sleeve is basted in first, and if the work is begun at the front sleeve seam. In this way, basting goes across the top of the sleeve first and then across the lower curve. With the thumbs against the sleeve side, the shaping in top of cap is retained easily. The right sleeve is then basted according to the same plan.

STITCHING SLEEVE INTO COAT

There are two choices as to the manner of holding coat and sleeve while the armscye line is being stitched. Each has its advantages.

The sleeve may be down, next to the feed dogs of the machine so that the coat side is up toward you. This method distributes the ease in the sleeve smoothly and allows you to watch to see that there is a clean-cut, smooth line of stitching on the coat side.

You may find it easier and more accurate to hold the coat down against the feed dogs and the sleeve side up toward you. You then watch the distribution of ease in the sleeve, but you must still have a smooth line of stitching on the coat side.

PRESSING ARMSCYE SEAMLINE

There are three choices for this according to the final effect desired. Custom tailors use Method 1 somewhat more often than Methods 2 or 3. Method 2 and Method 3 force some of the wool seam edges into an unnatural position so that they must be clipped or notched and pressed hard, or they will not maintain the position desired. Method 1 leaves a soft roll in sleeve cap. The second method gives a flat, hard-pressed seamline. Method 3 gives a hard-pressed, slightly bulky edge on the coat side.

Method 1. Do not press at all. In this case the seam edges across the top of the sleeve will turn into the sleeve and leave a soft, slight roll across the top.

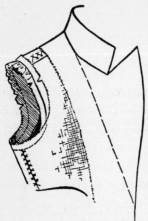

Seam edges should be graded. The seam edges across the underarm section will turn up toward the armpit.

Method 2. Press seam edges open around the top half of the armscye line. On the coat side, seam edges will have to be clipped to make them lie flat. On the sleeve side, seam edges will need more shrinking; also, notches will probably have to be cut so that this seam edge will lie flat. Seam edges across underarm section will turn up toward the armpit as in Method 1 (Fig. 41).

Method 3. Press both seam edges toward the body of the coat across top half of armscye line. Seam edge of coat will need clipping as in Method 2. Seam edge of sleeve may need a little more

Fig. 41

shrinking. In this method, the seam edges must be caught to position at the shoulder seamline of the coat. A catstitch may be used. Seam edges across underarm section will turn up as in Method 1 and 2.

TREATMENT OF REINFORCEMENT IN COAT AT ARMSCYE LINE

If Method 1 or 2 above is chosen, the edge of reinforcement may be loosely basted to the edge of wool seam. If Method 3 is used, baste the reinforcement close to the line of stitching. In all three cases, the raw edge of reinforcement extends beyond the line of stitching of the armscye line.

FINISHING LINING AT ARMSCYE LINE

This occurs after lining is placed in coat. See directions for "Lining," page 100.

HEMMING THE COAT

Hemline has been marked with marking basting.

CUTTING REINFORCEMENT FOR HEM

Cut bias of wigan ½″ to ¾″ wider than the finished hem.

CONSTRUCTION OF HEM OF COAT WITH CURVE AT LOWER FRONT EDGES

Place this bias strip so that ¼″ to ⅛″ of wigan extends below marking for hemline (Fig. 42). Some tailors prefer to have the cut edge of the bias strip just meet the marking for hemline. The latter makes less bulk but there is a little more danger of stretching the folded edge of the wool hem, either during construction or during the life of the garment.

Let the end of the strip lap under the front facing by ½″ or more (Fig. 42).

Using a long and short basting stitch with thread matching the wool, catch the bias reinforcement to the coat along the foldline. This stitching stays in the coat and so must not show from the right side (Fig. 42).

Turn hem and baste close to the fold. Shrink out any excess fullness at top of hem by using gathering thread and by steaming. If fullness falls close to a body seam, the seam may be ripped part way down to the hemline and the fullness removed by taking the seam deeper. Only slight

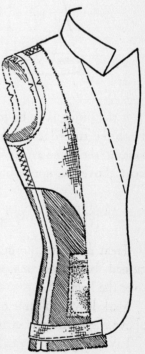

Fig. 42

fullness may be removed this way, for there is a tendency to give the lower hemline a slight point. Press the hem against wood.

Catstitch over the raw edge of the front facing and into the coat hem. Use fine stitches so that raw edge is well covered (Fig. 43).

If the lining is to be fastened down at hem, catstitch the hem to its reinforcement and fasten the reinforcement loosely to the coat by a slip stitch or catstitch (Fig. 43). Another satisfactory treatment is to machine stitch the wool hem to the reinforcement $1/8''$ from the upper raw edge of wool. Hold wool against feed dog of machine so that the wool is eased onto the bias reinforcement. The machine stitch gives a flat firm result, which is more or less desirable according to the type of wool fabric being used.

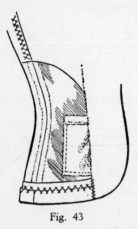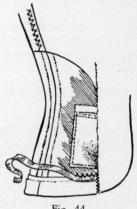

Fig. 43   Fig. 44

If the lining is to be loose, as is usual with long coats, use seam tape to finish the top edge of hem. Backstitch seam tape to reinforcement and coat hem at the same time. Trim reinforcement and catstitch tape loosely to coat above the upper line of hem (Fig. 44).

CONSTRUCTION OF HEM FOR JACKET OR COAT WITH STRAIGHT LINES FORMING A CORNER AT LOWER FRONT EDGE

Treat as above through the first steps, so that hem has been reinforced, turned, basted, shrunk, and pressed. Bring front facing into final position over the hem.

Mark lower foldline of facing so that the line is slightly (perhaps $1/8''$) above the foldline of coat hem.

Lay facing open away from the coat, but leave in position the lower foldlines of hem and facing.

Cut away excess material of hem and facing, leaving $1/2''$ seam allowance along lower foldlines of hem and facing, and leaving $1''$ allowance for facing to lap over vertical end of hem (Fig. 45).

With facing again in position, use a long and short slip stitch to hold facing to front reinforcement, throughout the length of coat from shoulder to hem.

Across the lower foldlines of hem and facing, slipstitch or fell fold of facing to foldline of coat hem. The foldline of facing will be slightly on the diagonal and slightly above hemline, so that it cannot show below hemline of coat (Fig. 46).

Between lower and upper lines of hem, the front facing still has a raw edge. This edge should not be turned under, but should be fastened to the

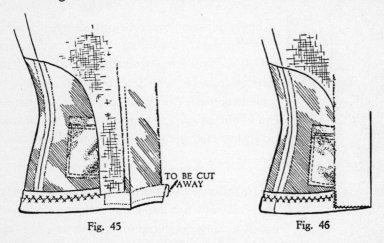

Fig. 45   Fig. 46

wool hem with a very fine catstitching over the raw edge and into the hem (Fig. 46).

If it is necessary to provide for lengthening the coat at some future time, the excess material between hem and facing should not be cut away. Failing to trim it away, however, makes front corners bulky and heavy. It is possible to cut away the excess material only from the facing. When coat is length-ened, only the facing needs to be pieced. This piecing will show but little, and not at all from right side of coat.

Pouches of pockets in long coats should be laid in place and loosely but securely fastened to reinforcement of the front. A swing tack or catstitch may be used. If the pouch lies between the reinforcement and lining of the finished coat, the bulge of the pocket will show less from the right side than it would if pouch lay between reinforcement and body of the coat.

TAILORED EYELET BUTTONHOLES

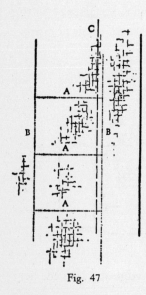

Fig. 47

POSITION OF BUTTONHOLES

Space buttonholes according to design of garment. Plan their length according to size of button. Cut a slit in a piece of waste fabric and slip button through it, in order to determine the length of buttonhole needed. Allow for sufficient space between end of buttonhole and edge of coat for the button to lie against coat and not too close to edge of coat.

MARKING

Use tailor's chalk with a very thin edge to mark a clear, narrow line for each buttonhole (Fig. 47, line A). Across each end of buttonhole, draw vertical line (Fig. 47, line B). Fig. 47, line C is the center front line of coat. The eyelet, triangular or round, will be centered on the center front line of coat (Fig. 48).

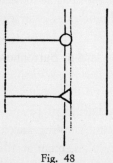

Fig. 48

Fig. 49

The line of buttonhole should be along a fillingwise grain.

PREPARATION OF COAT FOR BUTTONHOLES

After position of buttonholes is planned and marked, lay coat facing back out of the way. Cut a narrow rectangle or oval away from the reinforcement

90

of the coat front under each line of buttonhole.

Over this opening, lay a piece of firm, fine fabric such as fine silesia. Trim so that it extends beyond the opening and thus laps over reinforcement of coat by $\frac{1}{4}''$ to $\frac{1}{2}''$. Catstitch finely to hold silesia to reinforcement (Fig. 49).

Cutting away reinforcement and putting silesia in place are done so that buttonholes may be worked through silesia rather than through stiff, coarse reinforcement.

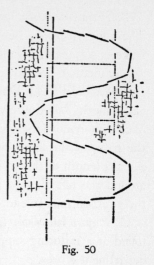

Fig. 50

Place coat facing back in its finished position. Use diagonal basting around each marking for buttonholes in order to hold together the coat, the reinforcement, and the facing. The basting is about $\frac{1}{2}''$ from line of button-hole (Fig. 50).

It may be a help to stitch a narrow rectangle around the marking for each buttonhole. This, too, holds three layers of fabric together. The rectangle should not be more than $\frac{1}{8}''$ wide. Such stitching makes a stiff buttonhole.

CUTTING

This is important and requires fine, sharp scissors.

Cut the length of buttonhole on a straight filling line, but not quite to the end near the edge of coat. This leaves space for the eyelet.

The eyelet at the end near edge of coat may be made in one of several ways, such as:

1. Cut away a small triangle with one straight edge parallel to edge of coat (Fig. 48).

2. Snip on very short lines radiating from end of buttonhole, and use a stiletto to round out the eyelet (Fig. 48).

PREPARATION OF BUTTONHOLE AND OF THREADS

A. *Prevent fraying of edges.* Edges may be overcast or they may be waxed to prevent fraying. To do the latter, warm a knife or small spatula, rub it quickly over a piece of beeswax, then over a piece of paper to remove excess wax. Then run knife through the opening of the buttonhole. Repeat if necessary, but be careful not to apply too much wax to the wool as it will leave a stain. Use light-colored wax for light-colored fabrics and dark wax for dark ones.

B. *Prepare stranding thread.* Buy a thread called gimp or prepare your own. The gimp is firmer, but the prepared thread is easier to work with and makes a softer buttonhole.

Use medium weight, preferably linen thread. Thread needle with about two yards of thread. Double it. Pull gently over beeswax; twist until firm and smooth. Rub down with hands to warm the wax and then with a piece of cloth to remove the excess. A tailor's technique is to hold the thread across the palm of the left hand and rub the right palm downward against it. A short length of thread is thereby warmed and twisted. Wrap this length around the left thumb. Repeat the rubbing on the next short length of thread. Continue to end of thread.

C. *Prepare buttonhole twist.* Use a twelve-strand twist, which is to be found at a tailoring supply house, or use size "D" twist, to be found in department stores.

Cut off a 27" length, draw it over beeswax and then between an absorbent cloth and warm iron. Waxing prevents curling and knotting of thread and makes a smooth, finished effect. Too much wax leaves stains on fabric.

MAKING THE BUTTONHOLE

A. *Strand the buttonhole.* With gimp or stranding thread in the needle, and with a knot at end, put needle into fabric ⅜" away from bar end of buttonhole;

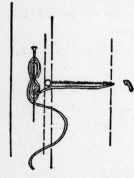

draw out again near bar end of buttonhole, leaving the knot on top of fabric (Fig. 51a).

Lay thread along buttonhole opening, close to edge. Hold it in place by wrapping it around a pin inserted in the fabric near the eyelet end of buttonhole. Strand lies flat, but not tight.

B. *Make the buttonhole stitch.* Hold the edge of the coat in the left hand, with eyelet end at the left. Fasten thread securely into fabric without a knot, and bring it out at the bar end of the buttonhole, which is the end farther from the front edge of coat.

Fig. 51a

Push needle through the opening at a right angle to it. Bring the needle out below the opening but push it only halfway through the fabric.

Pick up the double thread near eye of needle and pass it under the needle's point from right to left (Fig. 51b).

Pull the needle out from the fabric and draw up the thread almost to the end.

Now drop the needle or slide it back in the hand so as to leave thumb and index finger free. Grasp the thread 3″ or 4″ from the buttonhole, pull it upward, and so "set the purl" on top and yet at the very edge of the button-

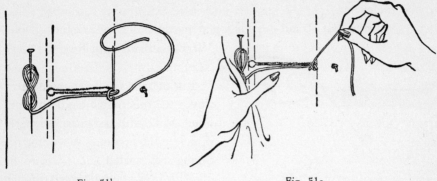

Fig. 51b   Fig. 51c

hole (Fig. 51c). This motion is an extra one when compared to the usual motion in making ordinary buttonholes. However, it is important for several reasons, which are readily seen during the work. Set-ting the purl completes the stitch. Now pick up the needle and repeat the stitch.

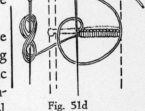

When four or five stitches have been made, remove the pin holding the stranding thread. Draw stranding thread until the knot at its end slips through the fabric and comes to a stop close to the bar end of the button-hole. The knot now lies under the top layer of wool

Fig. 51d

fabric and so is hidden. Now replace strand and wind around pin (Fig. 51d). Keep it in line with cut edge.

C. *Observe certain precautions.* Insert needle at right angles to the opening. Throw the double portion of thread under needle point from right to left.

"Set the purl" each time on top of cut edge.

Space stitches closely, yet not so close that there is too little room for the purl at the edge.

Begin at bar end of buttonhole.

Work from right to left.

Push needle through the opening, downward and toward you through the fabric.

Do not pull twist too tightly since the result is a hard, stiff edge.

D. *Work around the eyelet.* Plan arrangement of stitches to produce a smooth line. Set the purl a

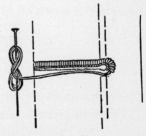

Fig. 51e

little farther away from the cut edge so that more stitches can be inserted, for it is the eyelet that receives the hardest wear (Fig. 51e).

Remove the pin holding the strand and let strand lie under stitches around the eyelet.

E. *Final steps.* Put strand in position along the other edge of buttonhole. Wrap it around a pin as before (Fig. 51e).

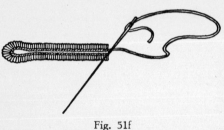

1. Continue the buttonhole stitch down the other edge of the buttonhole. Make the last stitch exactly opposite the first one, when buttonholing was started.

Fig. 51f

2. Bring needle and thread through the purl of the first stitch thus drawing the first and last purls closely together (Fig. 51f). Drop this needle and thread in order to do the next step.

3. Carefully draw up stranding thread to make buttonhole firm and smooth at edge. It can be drawn too tightly. Place a stiletto in the eyelet end

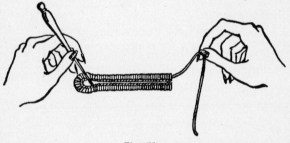

Fig. 51g

and hold it there as you draw up stranding thread (Fig. 51g). The use of stiletto prevents drawing thread too tightly and improves the appearance of the finished buttonhole.

Push the needle that carries the stranding thread through to wrong side of coat and fasten off firmly.

Fig. 51h   Fig. 51i

4. Across end of buttonhole, make a short bar by pushing needle down through the fabric at one edge of buttonhole and up through the fabric at the other edge. Needle should pass through fabric in a vertical line each time. Three or four stitches form this bar.

5. Work three or four purled stitches over the bar, setting the purl toward the buttonhole (Fig. 51i).

Push needle to wrong side and fasten off with one or two short stitches. The bar may be left without the purling stitches (Fig. 51h).

FALSE BUTTONHOLES

These may be used on sleeves with vents when there are worked buttonholes in the front opening of the coat. They are worked through the outside layer of wool and reinforcement only.

Use buttonhole twist and a fine chain stitch to outline the edges as of a regular buttonhole.

FIG. 52

Begin at the end nearer to the folded edge of the vent. Turn the stitches around the other end in order to produce an unbroken line around this end. Continue chain stitches down the second side of the buttonhole. Fasten thread off at the first end (Fig. 52).

The button is attached so as to cover the first end.

WEIGHTS FOR SHORT JACKETS

Weights of different sizes are available in department stores and tailoring supply houses. The choice depends upon the weight of wool fabric used and on the degree of downward pull desired.

Weights are usually too thick. They may be flattened by using a hammer and a hard, wood block. When they are to be flattened, you should buy a weight of small diameter.

Cover each weight with a piece of lining fabric without turning under the raw edges. Sew each one to the coat after the hem has been turned and sewed to the reinforcement. The placement of each weight depends upon the need to have a slight downward pull. Frequently the positions are at each side of center back and just back of each side seam. They are to be concealed by the lining when it is in place, therefore they are placed on the hem or seam just above the planned line of the lining.

LINING

CUTTING

Linings are usually cut from the same pattern as the coat, with a few changes suggested by pattern instructions. Depending upon design of coat, there may be a separate piece of pattern for the lining. If the coat is of intricate cut, there will be a separate pattern. Below are a few points to observe.

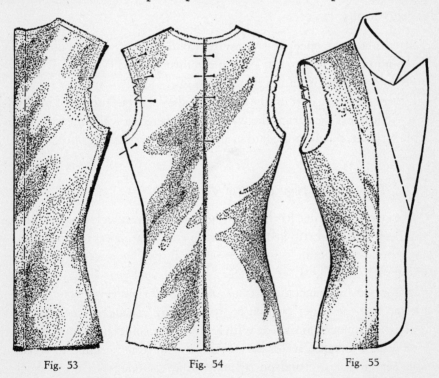

Fig. 53   Fig. 54   Fig. 55

Back. Often this is cut exactly as the coat is cut, except for allowing 1″ pleat in center back from neck to hem (Fig. 53). An easy way to handle the pleat is to baste it as if it were a tuck with the basting line on the center back. Baste the pleat flat and use the upper foldline as the center back (Fig. 54).

Front. This is often cut as the coat is cut, minus the front facing and plus at least 1″ for finishing. Let the front edge of the lining lie on warp grain clear to the shoulder. Later, a dart will be folded in for fitting to shoulder and bust, even if there was none in the coat (Fig. 55).

Body gore. This is cut exactly like the body gore of coat.

Length. The length can be cut 1″ shorter than the coat is cut. Even so, the finished lining will prove to be slightly longer than the finished coat, for the lining will be eased into the coat.

MARKING

Use chalk marks to mark seamlines. Darts should be marked, though they may not be stitched on these lines; in fact, small darts and the front shoulder dart are not stitched at all.

CONSTRUCTION

Stitch and press open all lengthwise seams. Do not stitch shoulder seams. Stitch no darts. Press center back pleat throughout its length. Remember upper fold of pleat is on the center back line.

If there are fitting darts at the waistline, they may be laid in and held with a catstitch across the dart at the waistline. If there is a waistline seam, as in a peplum jacket, the darts are laid in and held by the stitching of the waistline seam.

PUTTING THE LINING INTO COAT

The coat at this time has been finished and has been well pressed. Sleeves have been lined and stitched into coat. In adjusting lining to coat, the coat may be placed on table wrong side up, or it may be placed on dress form wrong side out. The latter is preferable. A second person may serve as a dress form, even though the coat may not fit her. The sleeves, too, are wrong side out and the upper portion of sleeve lining is hanging free.

Place the lining against coat with center backs coinciding. Watch so as to leave seam allowance across back neckline. Pin from neckline to waistline along center back. Fit and pin at under-arm seamline, then up to shoulder at each side. If there is a dart in the shoulder of the coat, it should be merely laid in, in the shoulder of the lining.

Fold front lining out of the way so that you may catch together the seam edges of coat and lining along the under-arm seam edges. Use a coarse thread and a long and short, loose basting. Leave 3″ or more free both at the top and at bottom of seamline. Hold lining easy against the wool (Fig. 56).

Bring front lining into position across the bustline. Turn under the front edge, place it over the edge of facing and pin at bustline. Lining is not taut crosswise of bust; it is slightly eased.

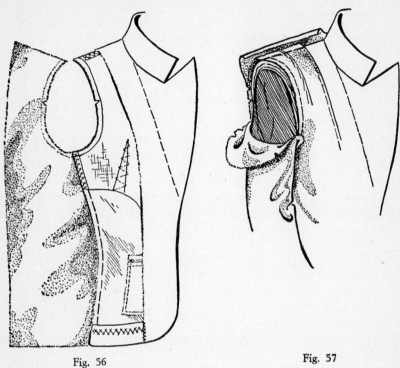

Fig. 56   Fig. 57

Fold in shoulder dart. Pin and tailor baste along dartline (Fig. 57). Since the front edge of lining follows line of wool facing, the front shoulder seam of lining is shorter than the back shoulder seam (Fig. 58).

Now, working from bustline upward, turn under front edge, keeping foldline of lining on warpline, if possible. If the front facing is quite curved, it is not possible to retain the warpline on the front edge of lining. The main consideration is to let the lining lie smoothly but easily through the bust, shoulder, and front edge (Fig. 59).

Baste lining of front shoulder seam to edge of wool seam or onto padding (Fig. 57). Do not turn under.

With long and short, loose basting, sew armscye seam edge of lining to wool seam edge or to shoulder padding (Fig. 58).

At this time it may be wise to try the coat on right side out and readjust the lining relative to the padding. The lining may prove too long. Right side out, the lining lies below (under) the padding; wrong side out it

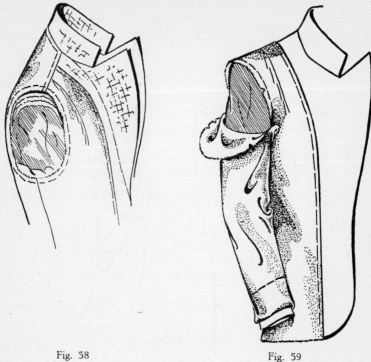

Fig. 58   Fig. 59

lies above (over) the padding. You are working with padding and lining upside down.

Turn under edge of back lining along neckline and back shoulder seam. Pin and baste (Fig. 58).

Across neckline, the lining laps over raw edge of top collar. Note that back shoulder seam is longer than front shoulder seam (Fig. 58). This extra length is near neck. It forms an angle at neck and shoulder lines. There is no such extra length if a wool facing is used across neckline of back.

Bring sleeve lining into place. Without using gathering threads, adjust ease along seamline in upper half of sleeve cap. Turn under seam allowance. Pin and baste across upper half of armscye line (Fig. 60). Adjust lower half of armscye line of sleeve to the armscye line of the coat lining. Notice that it is here that the extra length of the sleeve lining is needed, so that the lining may be easy as it passes over the bulk of the wool seam edges. (Figs. 61a and 61b). This step is easier to handle, if before adjusting the lower part of the armscye seam, the sleeves are turned right side out and if the work is done on the table. The lining is held easy throughout the armscye line; the actual fullness is only in the upper half.

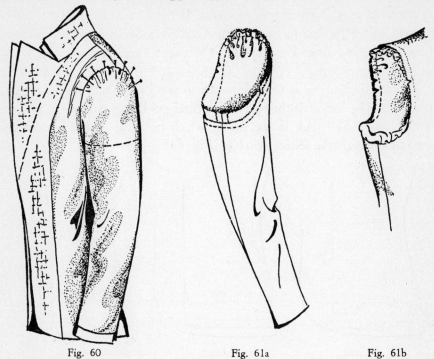

Fig. 60   Fig. 61a   Fig. 61b

ADJUSTING LINING TO HEM AT LOWER EDGE

Try coat on, right side out. Test carefully to find places where lining seems taut, or pulled. Release and re-pin or re-baste, as necessary.

A second person should pin coat and lining together along a horizontal line that is a few inches above hemline of coat. Remove coat and lay it flat on table, lining side up. Baste along line of pins (Fig. 62a). Ease lining below line of pins and pin again, parallel to first set of pins on a line near to upper edge of hem. The lining lies easy between the two rows of pins (Fig. 62a).

Turn under raw edge of lining ½" to ¾" and lay this folded edge over edge of wool hem, leaving 1" to 2" of wool hem showing. Short jackets have narrower wool hems than do long coats. Baste lining to hem ½" above folded edge of lining. This treatment is used when lining is to be fastened to coat along hemline (Fig. 62b).

If lining is to fall free from coat along hemline, finish lining with a 1" hem, so that lower edge of lining lies 1" to 2" above lower line of coat hem and fully covers the finish of the upper edge of wool hem.

SEWING LINING TO COAT

A slip stitch may be used. It gives a nice finish, but it is not highly durable. A hemming or felling stitch shows more, but it is more durable.

Fell or slipstitch across back neckline and both shoulder seams, down each front facing, and around armscye line. Wherever there is ease in the lining, distribute it smoothly.

If lining at hemline is to be fastened to wool hem, turn folded edge of lining back ¼″ and fell through one thickness of lining and into wool hem. This forms a ¼″ tuck in the lining which falls free at the bottom and entirely conceals the felling stitches (Fig. 62c).

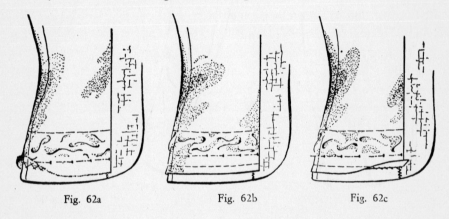

Fig. 62a   Fig. 62b   Fig. 62c

If lining is to fall free at hemline, fell the hem of lining. At each seamline, catch lining loosely to wool hem by making a swing tack.

The pleat in center back, the front shoulder darts, and other darts which were merely laid in without stitching are now finely catstitched. The line of catstitching runs crosswise of the pleats or darts 2″ or 3″ below the respective seamlines. The stitches pass through the lining only, and thus do not catch the wool.

A quick method of attaching lining is suggested here. It is satisfactory if you are sure that lining is of correct size and shape for coat.

Machine stitch the front lining pieces to the wool front facings, using a plain seam. Press seam edges toward the lining so that the wool edge is not turned back. This may be done either before or after the wool facing is attached to the coat.

When you are ready to attach the other pieces of lining, lay coat and front lining with right sides facing each other. Stitch the body seams of the lining.

Turn coat and lining with their right sides out. Finish shoulder and armscye seams as in the method above.

INTERLINING

Cut according to instructions on pattern.

Short jackets are not often interlined because of the added bulk. Long coats are frequently interlined. In general, the shape of interlining follows the design of the coat. Sometimes it is cut shorter at the bottom. Sometimes an inch or two at top of sleeve is cut away so as to reduce bulk in this area. In this case, the interlining does not enter the armscye seamline, so that there is danger that the interlining may drop and wrinkle near the upper edge.

MARKING

Mark darts, notches, and seamlines as with wool fabrics and lining.

CONSTRUCTION

There are two methods, each of which has its own advantages.

Method 1. Slash foldlines of darts, lap raw edges and catstitch together.

Lay each section of interlining against corresponding section of lining. Tailor baste the two together.

In joining seams, baste and stitch the four thicknesses together. Cut away the seam allowance of the interlining and press lining seams open.

This method is simple and it is quickly done. The results of it are slightly more bulky than those from the next method. Also, when coat needs relining, the interlining must be removed with the old lining and reinserted with the new one. This is not the case with Method 2.

Method 2. After the interlining is cut and marked, slash the dart lines, lap raw edges and catstitch the darts as in Method 1.

Place each piece of interlining against wrong side of corresponding section of wool coat.

Tailor baste to hold each in place, but leave a 3" or 4" space free near seamlines (Fig. 63).

Lay one edge of shoulder and one of underarm seam of interlining over the corresponding seam of wool coat.

Baste edges of interlining and of coat seam together with a coarse thread. Lay other edge of seam of interlining over the first edge (Fig. 63). Cat-stitch edges of interlining together (Fig. 64).

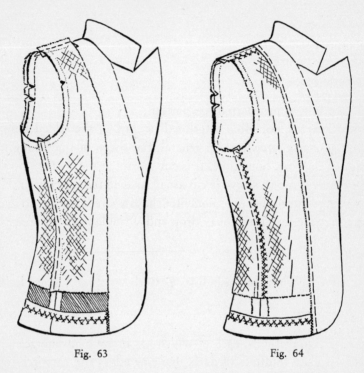

Fig. 63   Fig. 64

If interlining for sleeve was cut the same size and shape as the sleeve, place interlining against the wool and tailor baste to position. Treat the sleeve seams in the same way as side seams were treated.

The seam allowances of interlining may be cut away so that the raw edges of interlining just meet on the seamline of the wool. The raw edges are cat-stitched together and lightly caught into the wool seam. This treatment yields a nonbulky result, but it is not so strong.

For Methods 1 and 2. At neckline, interlining should be cut away to prevent bulk on this line. If neckline at back was finished with a wool facing, interlining may be slipped under edge of wool facing and held in place with an invisible long and short basting. Along front facing lines, interlining may be slipped under edge of wool facing and held in place with a long and short basting (Fig. 64).

At armscye line of coat the interlining should lie flat and the outer edge caught to the free edge of the reinforcement with a long and short basting.

The interlining of the sleeve is now brought into place along the armscye line.

The top of sleeve may be slashed and edges lapped in order to remove bulkiness of excess fullness.

Lap raw edge of interlining of sleeve over the free edge of interlining of coat along the armscye line and catstitch. The method is the same as for the other seams discussed above.

At hemline of sleeve, interlining is cut away just above the upper edge of wool hem. Its loose edge may then be basted to upper edge of reinforcement, or it may be caught only to the edges of the sleeve seams.

At hemline of coat, interlining may be cut several inches shorter than the coat, so that it does not enter the area of the hemline (Figs. 63 and 64). If Method 1 is used, the interlining may be cut nearly down to the foldline of the hem of the lining. In this case, the hem of the lining may be turned up over the interlining. The coat lining then is not felled to the wool coat. It is held in place by swing tacks.

PRESSING

There are many methods for pressing, and various tools and equipment for different methods. Below is one set of instructions using simple equipment. The method may be varied according to previous experience and present degree of skill.

A distinction should be made between shrinking and pressing. Shrinking may be exactly what the name implies, a shortening of length or width. The process is applied to wool fabric, as shown in the directions on "Preparation of Wool Fabric," page 8, in order to make uniform the length or the width of a piece of fabric. At the same time, the yarns of the fabric are brought back to their correct relationship of filling yarns at right angles to warp yarns. Shrinking has another purpose at times, namely, to change the shape of the fabric, as at the top of a sleeve cap. In this, warp and filling yarns converge along the line of greatest shrinkage.

Pressing aims only to restore the original texture of fabric and garment, or to set a new creaseline, as at the edge of a pleat or along the stitching line of a seam. In so doing, it usually aims to maintain the right-angle relationship of warp and filling threads in the body of the garment.

Both shrinking and pressing should leave the surface texture and appearance of the fabric unchanged.

Overshrinking or overpressing causes undesirable results, such as pebbly, rough surface on smooth fabric, or shiny spots on dull fabric, or crushed nap on napped fabrics.

EQUIPMENT

A. *Pressing iron.* The usual weight and size of iron is sufficient for satisfactory work.

B. *Pressboards and cushion.* The usual type of ironing board should be well padded.

For pressing curved surfaces, such as bust and shoulder area, a ham cushion is essential. It is shaped like a ham with one large and one smaller end. It is filled in order to produce a hard, almost unyielding surface. It may be made of two pieces of heavy cotton fabric, such as drilling, stitched together and filled with cotton batting or sawdust. A usable size is indicated in Fig. 65.

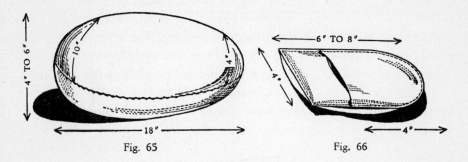

Fig. 65   Fig. 66

A small hand pad that may be fitted into the top of a sleeve is a help. It has a strap or pocket into which the hand may be slipped while pressing (Fig. 66).

Like the ham cushion, it is made of two pieces of fabric stitched together. A third piece of fabric, only 4″ long may be stitched with the first two, so that it forms a pocket into which the hand may be slipped.

A seam board may be made from a magazine, rolled tightly and covered with fabric (Fig. 67a). By laying it on the pressboard, and then laying a straight length of seam along the curved top, a seamline may be pressed

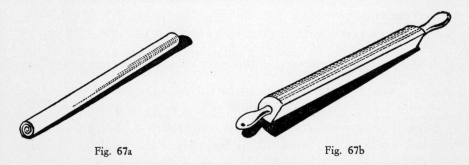

Fig. 67a   Fig. 67b

without danger of the edge of seam marking the body of the fabric. Since this board is usable in many ways, a more durable one may be wanted. If so, a rolling pin cut in half lengthwise is an excellent base for firm padding and tight covering. Since it has a flat base, it does not roll on the board during the pressing (Fig. 67b).

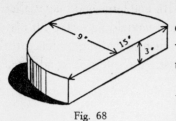

Fig. 68

An uncovered surface of hard wood is an essential. Pressing against wood leaves the wool surface flat and the surface appearance unchanged. It may be merely a thick ($\frac{7}{8}''$ to $1''$) plank about 15" by 8" or 9". Or it may be shaped like a cheese. It is then called a cheese block. The cheese block has both flat and curved surfaces for different needs in pressing. The measurements for a small one are suggested in Fig. 68. For long-time use, the wood should be treated so as to prevent warping and to prevent possible staining of fabric.

C. *Beater and press cloths.* The beater or clapper is a small wooden tool especially helpful in pressing seams flat or in flattening faced edges as on lapels or collar. It is like a heavy paddle (Fig. 69). To use it, lightly steam

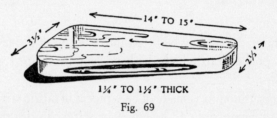

1¼" TO 1½" THICK

Fig. 69

the seam or edge to be pressed. While the fabric is still steaming, beat or clap it with the beater to force out the steam and to flatten the fabric. It is often used with a wood pressboard so that the fabric lies on wood and is beaten with a wooden clapper.

There is a variety of cloths, usable in numerous ways. A cloth serves several purposes: to protect the wool fabric from too much heat; to provide for application of moisture; to distribute a small amount of moisture evenly over the wool fabric; to provide a surface that will leave the wool fabric unchanged in surface appearance. All cotton used must be entirely free from starchy dressing. Lintless fabrics are best. Drilling is good.

A most satisfactory type of cloth is made of two pieces of fabric, one of lightweight wool and one of mediumweight cotton. The two may be stitched together. The wool side is laid against the wool fabric during pressing. Moisture may be applied by sponging the cotton side lightly or by laying on top of the cotton side a cotton cloth wrung out of water. However the moisture is applied, a dry cotton cloth is laid on top. The dry one protects the hands from the possibility of steam burns and causes better distribution of steam as it reaches the wool fabric.

All this may seem involved, but good pressing is one of the most important processes in tailoring. With little experience, but with much care, excellent pressing may be done. In fact, home pressing is often better than that done by a tailor on a homemade product.

PROCEDURE FOR PRESSING

Lay garment right side down on pressboard or cushion or wood. Adjust garment so that for flat surfaces grainlines are at right angles to each other; and for curved surfaces the coat fabric lies over the curved cushion as it is to be pressed.

Lay the wool and cotton, the damp and dry cloths over the coat fabric, as indicated above.

Test the iron for degree of heat necessary to produce steam without scorching dry cotton cloth.

Lower iron onto press cloth lengthwise of the warpwise grain of fabric. Lift before imprint of iron can be left on fabric. Repeat the "lower-and-lift" motion, always with an overlapping of areas covered by the iron. On curved surfaces, the iron may be "rocked" over the curve. Lift all the press cloths frequently in order to let out steam accumulating in the wool fabric.

Do not press until coat fabric is dry, but leave a small amount of steam in it. At end of pressing, hang garment carefully, since it is slightly damp and therefore will wrinkle or stretch easily. As it dries, it will take the shape that was planned by the pressing and by the method of hanging it after pressing.

PROCEDURE FOR SHRINKING

To retain length or width and to maintain right-angle relationship of warp and filling threads:

Lay wool fabric on flat pressboard in position desired for final product. This position leaves the wool puffy or ripply in spots. Pat out so as to distribute the puffiness.

Do not use a wool press cloth. Use a heavy cotton one next to the wool fabric, then a dampened one, then a dry one.

Lower the iron just enough to produce steam. Apply no pressure with the iron. Lift and lower iron along lengthwise grain of fabric with overlapping of areas touched by the iron. Do not lift press cloths until after small area has been steamed.

Lift press cloths and see if wool fabric is sufficiently shrunk. If it is, finish with a light pressing. If it is not fully shrunk, repeat the procedure. It is better to shrink the wool gradually by repeating the process than to shrink it quickly in one process.

To produce a curved surface and thus change right-angle relationship of warp and filling threads:

Use two or three parallel rows of gathering threads along edge of curved area as along the seamline of top of sleeves (Fig. 30) page 77. For shrinking, these are best put in by using a hand-running stitch; the finer the stitch, the easier the shrinking will be. One row of gathering is exactly on the seamline, one is ⅛″ outside of it, and one row is ⅛″ inside of it, when three threads are used. When two threads are used, one is on the seamline and one is ⅛″ outside of seamline.

Draw gathering threads up until fabric is in the shape desired. Fasten thread ends.

Lay curved surface over ham cushion. Pat out gathers so as to distribute fullness.

Apply press cloths and iron in order to produce a very light steaming. Lift cloth to make sure no wrinkles are forming along gathered edge on body of fabric. As soon as curved edge begins to hold the shape desired, snip the gathering thread, if there is one that lies inside the seamline, and remove it. If it were left beyond this point, it would leave a pressing mark that is hard to remove.

The seam edge of the wool fabric will form little darts which should not be firmly pressed. This seam edge may be treated later after the seam is stitched. The essential part of this shrinking is in the area that will show in the finished coat.

Leave the fabric moist as with pressing, but let it dry over a curved surface. The shoulder pad may provide the curved surface wanted for the sleeve top or the ham cushion for curve of coat front through the bust and armscye area.

When thoroughly dry, apply a light pressing.

ADDITIONAL SUGGESTIONS

In pressing seams, "finger pressing" is an easy means of opening the seam edges. Lay the seam on the seam board; moisten the fingers lightly as on a wet sponge; pat the seam edges open with damp fingers. In doing this, moisture, pressure, and heat are being applied by the fingers. When edges are separated, the usual pressing may be done.

Steaming followed by beating with the clapper is good for seams.

In pressing seams or pleats, a mediumweight paper cut into a 2″ wide strip may be laid between the seam edge or fold of pleat and the body of the garment. Then the usual pressing may be done. The paper keeps seam edge or pleat from leaving a pressmark on right side of garment. In shrinking out fullness from a hem as at bottom of coat, lay a heavy paper between hem and body of coat.

PRESSING A JACKET OR COAT

This pressing is done when the wool coat is completed but the lining is not yet inserted. Sleeves have been stitched in but the sleeve lining is free at the armscye.

EDGE PRESSING

Press on wood with right side (the outside) of garment against wood. Use press cloths as above. Give a hard press. Do not stretch any of the edges. Begin with left side of coat at topmost button with facing uppermost.

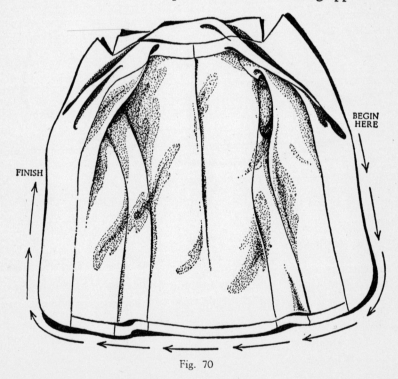

Fig. 70

Work down the front edge.
Continue around hemline with the right side still down against wood.
Work up the right-hand side of coat to the topmost buttonhole (Fig. 70).

Turn the coat over so that it is right side up, ready for pressing lapel edges.

Start with left side of coat at topmost button, and press lapel.

Continue around edge of collar and down edge of lapel on right-hand side (Fig. 71).

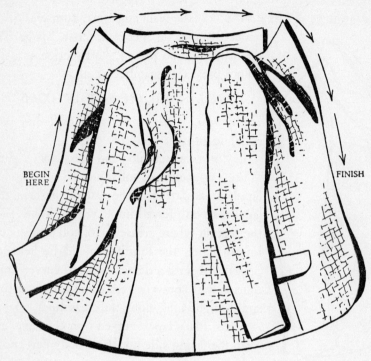

Fig. 71

Lay lapel and collar into position and press creaseline of collar *only from the inside.*

BODY PRESSING

Press on ham cushion with right side of coat up. Use press cloths as before. Give only a very light press. Be careful not to alter any of the shaping.

Lay top of coat at small end of ham cushion, beginning on left-hand side of coat. Press in this order:

Left shoulder
Left underarm
Left pocket
Left lower front
Left lower back
Left upper back.

Continue around right-hand side of coat, reversing the order outlined above.

SHOULDER PRESSING

Press shoulder seamline lightly.

Use hand pad to press curved portion of sleeve cap. Since pad is small, it is all too easy to overpress the cap and leave it rippled.

Press armscye seamline. The way the seam edges may turn was discussed under "Replacing Sleeve in Coat," page 85. Use the hand pad and press a short section at a time or do not press this seamline at all.

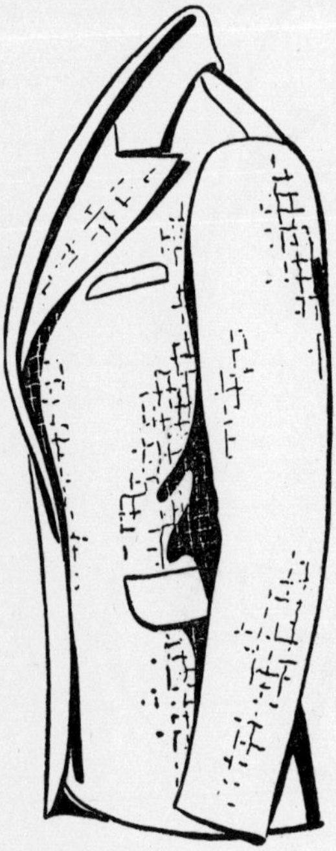

FINAL FINISH ON FACE OF COAT

Collar. Lay paper between coat and edge of collar to protect body of coat.

Lay over ham cushion and press from right side.

Press creaseline of collar and 1" of creaseline on lapel but no farther. The rest of the creaseline in lapel is never pressed into a crease. When pressing the section where creaseline of collar meets creaseline of lapel, the foldline should be held on the pressboard with a definite inward curve. This precaution will prevent stretching and tend to a desirable tightening along the creaseline.

Lapels. Place lapel, curved over the ham cushion, with the facing side up. Press body part, not edge of lapel.

Fig. 72

Remove from cushion. Hold ends of creaseline and pull gently along creaseline. This helps to set the roll of the lapel so that it is not necessary to press a fold along the creaseline.

Fig. 72 indicates a well-pressed jacket.

PRESSING OF LINING

This is done with the coat laid on the board with the lining right side up. Use a mediumweight, *dry* press cloth and an iron that is just warm, not hot.

Press the edges of the lining where they are felled to the wool coat.

Along the under half of the armscye line, press so that the lining of sleeve rolls up and over the wool seam edges which stand up into the armscye.

Turn the sleeve liningside out, press the lower edge lightly. Use the hand pad inside the sleeves.

BUTTONS

PREPARATION

Coat and facing are in place.

Lining is attached, if button thread is to pass through facing.

Lining is not attached, if button thread is to pass through coat wool and reinforcement, but not through facing.

Better results are obtained if coat is completely finished and pressed for the last time before buttons are attached.

MARKING

Coat should be in correct position on the wearer.

Front opening should be pinned together.

Location of buttons is marked with a pin passed through buttonhole. This mark should be on the basting line which marks the center front.

Thread-mark the location of each button.

ATTACHMENT

Use heavy thread to match button or coat wool. There is thread called button thread or cord; buttonhole twist may be used. The latter may be lightly waxed.

Use a small knot at end of thread.

Take a small stitch on right side of coat on the point marked for button. Draw knot close to fabric and pull it through one layer of wool, so as to conceal it. Take a second stitch in same place.

Run thread through button, either the eye or shank type, and then through fabric.

Provide for shank or stem of thread by placing a pin, match, or pencil in the loop of thread already formed. Size of pin, match, or pencil depends on bulkiness of fabric.

Sew through button and through fabric, always over the pin, match or pencil, until there are enough strands for durability (Fig. 73a). Bring thread to surface of fabric under the button.

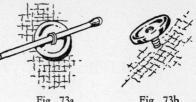

Fig. 73a   Fig. 73b

Remove pin or pencil. Wind thread around strands between button and fabric. This winding should be regular and firm so as to leave a sturdy, even stiff, neat thread shank (Fig. 73b).

Fasten thread firmly into coat fabric and cut off.

Even a button made with a shank needs at least a short thread shank or it may cause the buttonhole to spread open while the coat is being worn.

SUGGESTIONS

For heavy duty coats, a small button may be placed under the button and against the facing. When using it, sew through the coat button and through this small reinforcing button with each stitch. The pin, match, or pencil then lies between the outer button and the right side of coat fabric.

Sewing through coat and facing provides for greater durability, but the stitches show on the facing side. The stitches that show should be short and neatly taken. The fabric should not pucker under the stitches.

Sewing through coat and reinforcement but not through facing provides for less durability, but stitches cannot show on the facing side since threads do not pass through the facing.

A common error is to wind the thread shank too loosely.

Note suggestions above for tightness and smoothness of winding.

QUALITIES OF A WELL-MADE GARMENT

These are a few points that frequently indicate a well-made garment.

GRAIN LINE OF FABRIC

Warplines are vertical in center front and center back and in the center of each sleeve when viewed from the side.

Filling lines are horizontal across bust, across width of back, across sleeve at a place in line with the bustline.

LOOSELY FITTED COAT

Slight, soft folds, often called blades of fabric, fall vertically in each of the following positions:

At each side of the front, from the armscye, so as to form silhouette lines of the front.

At each side of the back from the armscye, so as to form silhouette lines of the back.

At each side of the sleeve from the armscye, so as to form silhouette lines when the sleeve is seen from a direct side view.

TRIMLY FITTED JACKET

Instead of the slight folds falling vertically in the front and back of a coat, there is a rounded curve from bust to armscye in front of jacket. There is a similar slight curve in back from shoulder to armscye. These curves have been formed by the "holding in" and darting at the armscye of front and back in the wool, the reinforcement, and the first layer of padding.

COLLAR

The creaseline fits snugly to neck across the back and over the shoulder.

Along the neckline, the collar fits trimly but comfortably where it passes over top of shoulder. If there is a feeling of tightness or weight along this

Notice curve of
fabric through
bust and underarm
in figure - left

Note blade of fabric
falling from armscye
in figure - right

Top figure shows ease of fit through waist and hipline.

- Notice the snugness of the collar, gentle roll of the lapel and the concealed seams of the front edge of center figure.

- The figure at the left shows matching of warp and filling lines of sleeve as related to the jacket.

line, the shoulder seam has not been curved to fit the curve of shoulder and base of neck, or the undercollar is not attached correctly.

Fall of collar lies flat against undercollar and coat, and fully covers the stand of collar.

Ends of collar lie flat, without curling.

LAPELS

There is a soft roll along the creaseline without an actual crease being pressed in on this line.

Lapels lie in position without curling of edges or points; seamlines along outer edges are concealed.

The lapels hold their position easily so that there is no bulge or broken line along the "V" of the front opening.

FRONT EDGES

Seams at edges are concealed.

Corners or curves at lower ends lie smooth without curling.

SLEEVES

Lines of silhouette, seen from front, back, and side views, fall vertically from top of sleeve to elbow. Lines from elbow to wrist easily follow lines of arm. Lower edge line is longer in back than across top of wrist.

WAIST AND HIP AREA

Waist and hip areas of fitted jacket have a smooth, easy fit so that there are no crosswise or diagonal wrinkles due to waist or hip being too tightly fitted.

A straight coat with trim lines falls over the hips easily, barely touching them. A coat with full lines does not touch the hips.

LOWER HEM LINE

No obvious line of stitches shows at top of wool hem.

There are no "pulled" spots due to lining being drawn too tight. Lining is not visible from right side of coat.

PLAIDS, STRIPES, OR CHECKS

The design of the fabric is carried across parts of the jacket or coat and across seamlines or openings according to the plan made in the pattern layout on fabric. The plan may be obvious, as it usually is with plaids, or it may be subtle as in the case of medium or small checks. In either case, the plan and its execution add to the final effect of the coat.

SUMMARY AND SUGGESTIONS

The most important parts of a jacket as far as general appearance is concerned are included in the area above the bustline. The collar lies smoothly and snugly against the neck. The creaseline of collar and foldline of lapel form an unbroken line that runs from the top button upward, around back of neck and down to the top buttonhole. The edges of lapels lie flat and the whole area of lapels curve softly over the bust. The shoulders and tops of sleeves give trim silhouette lines. This entire section of the jacket looks as if it "belonged" to the wearer.

If some detail of fit or construction is not satisfactory, the worker should refer to the directions for that detail. Re-reading the instructions may reveal an error in the work and point the way to correcting it.

• Notice ease of the jacket at the waistline and the hipline—right

• Left—observe matching the design of the fabric.

FLY FRONT FOR COATS

Fly fronts are easy to make if you have a general idea of the processes involved. The fly extends only part way down the front, usually from the lower end of the lapel to a point below the hipline. This section of the right-hand side of the front of the coat is faced. This section of the wool facing also is faced. After each is faced, the front facing is applied to the front of the coat and the two (facing and coat front) are stitched together above the fly and below the fly. That means that the facing and the front are not stitched together throughout the length of the fly. The left side of the coat front is finished only with a wool facing as usual, and according to the directions given in "Front Facing," page 54.

Fig. 74

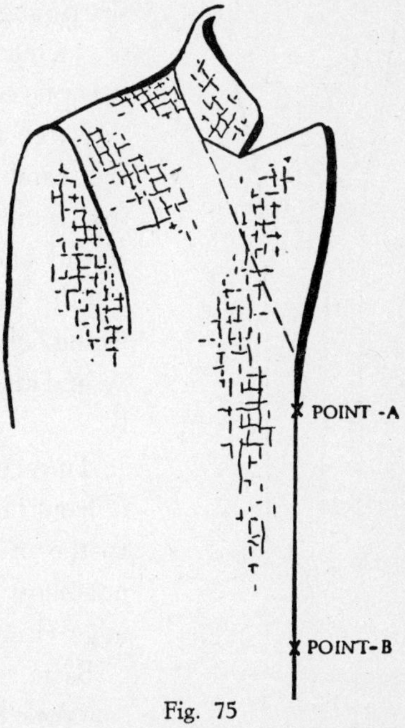

CUTTING

The coat front and the facing for it are cut as usual.

Cut two pieces of wool fabric on warpwise grain about 20″ long by 3″ wide. The ends are on a decided slant

Fig. 75

so that the sharp end extends beyond the other by 2½″ (Fig. 74). These two pieces will form facings for the front edge of coat and for the coat front facing throughout the length of the fly opening.

MARKING

The seamlines of coat front and front facing have been marked.
Mark ½″ seam allowances on each edge of each facing piece.

121

Lay coat front, front facing, and the two facing pieces together so as to mark each of the four pieces at two points. One point (A, in Figs. 75, 76) is where the stitching will end at the upper end of the fly, and the other is where the stitching will end at the lower end of the fly (B, in Figs. 75, 76). These two points are on the seamline of the facing pieces and on seamline of front edge of coat and of coat facing. If these points are accurately marked, the rest of the work will seem simple.

CONSTRUCTION

Lay one piece of facing against the coat front facing for the right-hand side of the coat. Right sides are together, the two points A are coinciding and the two points B are coinciding. Note that the sharp angle at the upper end of facing points upward when it is placed on the facing.

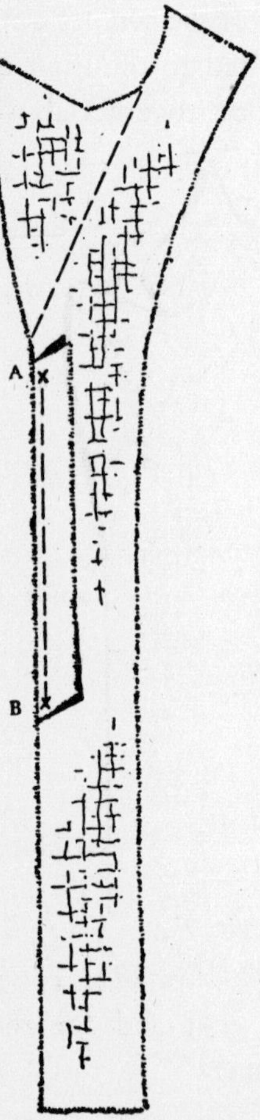

Stitch the two together along the seamline planned and exactly from point A to point B. Fasten thread ends securely (Fig. 76).

Clip the seam edge on the coat facing only, from the edge to point A, and also from the edge to point B.

Turn facing strip to wrong side of front facing. Roll the seam ¹⁄₁₆" to the inside so that facing does not show at all on the finished edge (Fig. 77).

Baste and press.

Work buttonholes through the two thicknesses of fabric. The end buttonholes should be about 3" from points A and B each (Fig. 77).

If fabric needs reinforcement for buttonholes, lay a strip of rein-forcement fabric between coat facing and facing strip. It should be cut warpwise and lie inside the seamlines between the two pieces of wool.

Fig. 76

Fig. 77

Lay the other piece of facing against the right-hand side of the front of coat. Right sides are together, and again points A are coinciding, and points B are coinciding.

Again the sharp end of facing points upward on the coat front.

Stitch the two together along the seamline planned and exactly from point A to point B. Fasten thread ends securely.

Clip the seam edge to point A and point B, respectively, and in the coat front only (not in the facing).

Turn facing strip to wrong side of coat front. Roll the seam edge to the

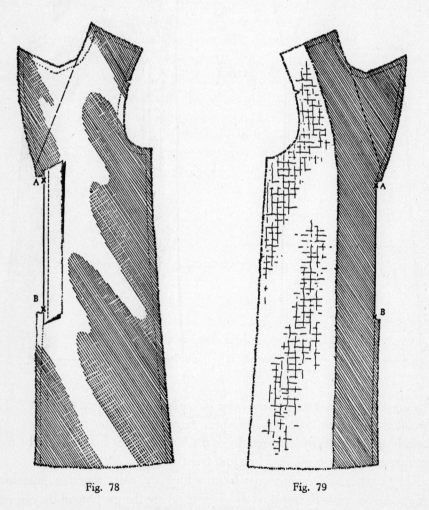

Fig. 78   Fig. 79

inside so that facing does not show at all on the finished edge. Baste and press (Fig. 78).

If the front edge of the coat is to have a surface or top stitching along the edge, it must be put in now, through front and facing strip, but only from point A to point B.

By this time, the front facing of the coat has been faced with one strip of

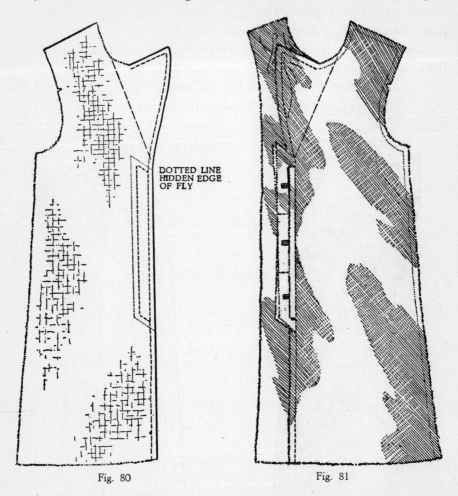

DOTTED LINE
HIDDEN EDGE
OF FLY

Fig. 80   Fig. 81

facing and the seam edge of the front facing has been clipped to point A and point B. Also, the coat front has been faced in a similar manner, and top stitching along the fly has been done, if the whole coat front was to be top-stitched. Now you are ready to join front facing to coat front.

Lay coat facing against coat front with right sides together, matching point A and point B, respectively. This is where the purpose of the clipped seam edge becomes clear. Baste from point A upward around the lapel and from point B downward along the edge of coat front (Fig. 79).

Stitch the two together, exactly on the seamline planned, ending each stitching exactly on the respective points A and B. Fasten threads securely at these two points. Grade seam edges as usual and turn facing to wrong side of coat front. Above point A, roll the seam edge toward the coat, not toward the facing, if the coat has a lapel. Below point B, roll the seam edge toward the facing. In each case, the purpose is to roll the seam over the edge so that the bulky seam does not show on the edge. Baste and press (Fig. 80).

Draw the coat front out of the way so that you may stitch through three thicknesses only, the coat front facing and the two strips of facing. Stitch crosswise midway between each two but-tonholes. These stitchings are parallel to the lines of buttonholes and run from the finished edge of coat to the raw edges of facings. They serve to hold the coat front smoothly in place when the coat is being worn. Fasten thread ends securely (Fig. 81.)

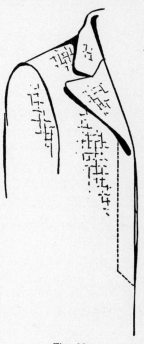

Replace the coat front in relation to the facing strips and front facing. Baste the four thicknesses together. Mark the coat front to correspond to the planned seamlines on the two strips of facing. This marking goes across the upper end of the strips, down the inside edge, and across the lower end (Fig. 82). If there was a top stitching along the front edge, this marking begins and ends on that line of stitching (Fig. 80). Topstitch according to marking lines. Fasten thread ends securely.

Fig. 82

If there was top stitching along the edge of coat front, it may now be con-tinued above and below the ends of the fly opening (Fig. 80).

UNLINED JACKETS

The choice of fabric is important. Fabric should have body and firmness, for there will be little or no reinforcement in the jacket, which would help the garment to hold its shape during wear. Some degree of thickness or bulk, also, is desirable. A careful rereading of "Selection of Fabric," page 4, may be of help.

The choice of design is equally important. The design should be simple; pieces of the garment should be cut with the warp grainlines in the usual relationship to pattern and to body of wearer. That is, the warplines should run up and down on each pattern piece, and thus be vertical when on the wearer of the jacket. The type of design should allow for an easy, soft fit; it should not require a close, snug fit.

PREPARATION OF WOOL FABRIC AND OTHER SUPPLIES

Follow directions as given previously under that title, page 6.

SHAPING COAT FRONT AND COAT BACK

In general, the directions previously given are applicable here. The chief difference is that there is little shaping done. The design chosen should be such that only slight shaping is needed.

The shoulder dart is pressed over the ham-shaped cushion, so that the area over the bust is somewhat curved. The armscye seamlines are eased in along the lower curves of back and front of jacket. The method is the same as in "Shaping Coat Front," page 26. The top of the sleeve cap is shaped according to previous directions under "Sleeves."

POCKETS

Flap and welt pockets are not satisfactory in this type of jacket. Patch pockets are better both from the standpoint of suitability of design and of satisfaction during wear. Two methods of preparing them are discussed here.

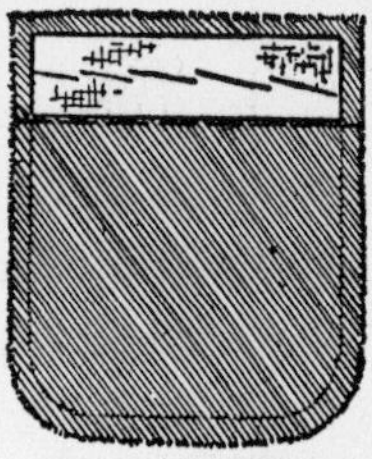

The unlined patch pocket. Cut the pocket with an allowance for a hem across the top and with seam allowances on the other edges (Fig. 83a). Or cut with seam allowances only on all the edges. In the latter case, cut an extra piece of fabric for a facing across the top of the pocket.

Fig. 83a

Cut a piece of reinforcement fabric, such as wigan or muslin, which is the exact size of the hem or facing without its seam allowances (Fig. 83a).

Place the reinforcement against the wrong side of the hem allowance or the facing and tailor baste it into place (Fig. 83a). Turn the seam edge of hem or facing along the line which will be the lower one when the jacket is being worn. This may be catstitched to the reinforcement, or the folded edge may be stitched. Press this edge (Fig. 83b).

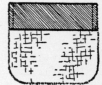

Fig. 83b

Turn the whole hem allowance down against the right side of the pocket, or lay the right side of the facing against the right side of pocket. This double layer of fabric is now treated so that the underlayer (which is the hem in the one case, and the facing in the other) is made slightly smaller than the outer layer. To do this, ease the outer layer against the underlayer and tailor baste the two together. Stitch across the two ends of the hem or facing (Fig. 83c).

Fig. 83c

Turn right sides out. The seamlines at the ends will be slightly rolled toward the wrong side of pocket because the outside layer was eased. Finish the first fold of hemline or of facing, either by hand or by machine (Fig. 83d).

Turn under the seam allowances on the other edges of pocket, baste and press lightly. Trim the seam edges to $3/16''$ or even less, if the fabric is firm (Fig. 83d).

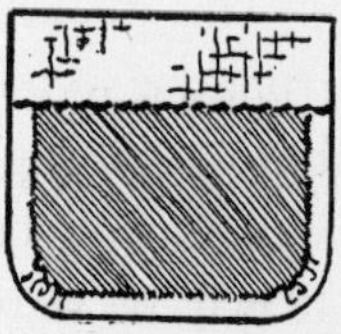

Place the pocket in position on the jacket. Tailor baste twice through the body of pocket. Baste the edges down to the jacket and then stitch.

Fig. 83d

The method of stitching pocket to jacket may serve both as decoration and as a finish for the seam edges inside of the pocket (Figs. 83e, f, and g).

The lined patch pocket. Cut pocket with a hem allowance across the top and seam allowances on other edges. Cut a lining piece with seam allowances

Fig. 83e

Fig. 83f

Fig. 83g

Fig. 83h

on all edges but smaller than the pocket by the amount allowed for the hem (Fig. 83h).

Reinforce the hem area as above (Fig. 83h).

Stitch the lining piece to the pocket piece along the first fold of the hem. Press the seam edges open (Fig. 83h).

Fold pocket and lining with right sides together and with the line of fold along the top line of pocket. Tailor baste the two together about 1″ from the raw edges. Now ease the wool fabric of the pocket against the lining fabric between the tailor basting and the raw edges. Baste again so as to hold the ease in place (Fig. 83i). Stitch around the pocket and lining edges. Leave a space open along the lower edge of pocket so that the whole piece may be turned right side out. It is equally good to leave such an opening where the lining was stitched to the first fold of the hem of the pocket.

Turn pocket right side out. Finger press the turned edges so that the seamline is surely rolled slightly toward the wrong side of the

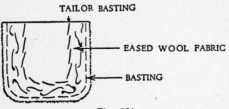

TAILOR BASTING

EASED WOOL FABRIC

BASTING

Fig. 83i

pocket. Baste. Finish by hand the opening left for turning pocket. Press. Place pocket in position on jacket and tailor baste through the center. Baste the outer edges to the jacket.

This pocket may be attached to jacket by hand stitches which are taken from the wrong side of jacket. They pass through the seam edges of pocket but not through the outside surface of pocket. It may be attached by machine stitching in one of several lines, as suggested for unlined patch pocket. It may be stitched ¼″ or more inside of pocket edge since the edge is a finished one.

Since the two upper corners of the pocket receive considerable strain, the method of attaching pocket to jacket should be planned for durability. The lines of machine stitching indicated in Figs. 83e, f, and g provide some degree of durability. It is possible to place a strip of lining fabric or silesia against the wrong side of the jacket and directly under the top of the pocket. This strip is longer than the top of the pocket and about 1″ wide. It is basted to position before the pocket is stitched to the jacket, so that the machine stitching holds it in place. The edge of this strip may be pinked or the edges may be folded under and stitched before the strip is placed in the jacket. If such a reinforcement is used, it should be inconspicuous in color and texture, since there will be no jacket lining to conceal it.

REINFORCEMENT

The body of the coat is reinforced under the front facings and lapels. The fabric used should not be stiff because it would make too much contrast between the front facings and the body of the jacket. Wigan or medium-weight muslin is satisfactory. (See "Preparation of Wool Fabric and Other Supplies," page 6).

Cutting and attaching. Cut reinforcement the same size and shape as the wool facing. Place it against the wrong side of the body of the jacket and tailor baste it into position.

Run a fine basting along the creaseline of the lapel, holding the two layers together.

LAPEL

Follow directions for taping the creaseline, as given under the topic, "Lapel," page 48.

Follow directions for taping lapel and front edges under the same topic, "Lapel," page 48. This step may be omitted in an unlined jacket. If it is omitted, trim the reinforcement close to the stitching which joins wool facing to jacket (See "Front Facing," page 54).

BOUND BUTTONHOLES

Follow previous directions, page 50.

FRONT FACING

Follow previous directions, page 54. If lapel and front edges were not taped, stitch through reinforcement, wool jacket, and wool facing. Trim seam edge of reinforcement as close to the line of stitching as possible. The rest of the previous directions may be followed.

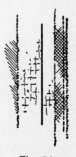

Fig. 84a

The inside edge of front facing may be finished with a bias tape in the same way as seams are finished. (See "Seams" below and

Fig. 84a.) The tape should cover raw edges of reinforcement and facing.

If seams are finished by turning and stitching raw edges as suggested below, trim the reinforcement under the facing so that the edge of wool facing may be turned over the edge of reinforcement. Stitch this folded edge.

SEAMS

Seams not only need to be flat, as in any jacket, but they need a neat, durable finish. Also, they should be so treated that the seam edges will hold their position throughout the life of the jacket.

Wherever the design of the garment makes it possible, use a plain seam with edges pressed open. This is usually possible in the vertical seams of body and sleeve. A different treatment is desirable in the armscye line.

Do not clip seam edges on curved seamlines as you would in a lined jacket. Stretch or shrink the seam edges so that they will lie flat against the body of the jacket. If it is difficult to make them lie flat, trimming the seam allowance to a narrower width may help. After pressing open, finish each seam edge. It is important to finish the edges of each seam as soon as the seam has been stitched and pressed. In other words, baste, stitch, press, finish, and again press each seam as you proceed.

Bindings are a satisfactory seam finish. Bias tape is easier to use than the straight-grain seam binding. Ready-made bias tape may be used, although it is often easier to handle bias strips cut from lining fabric. These strips should not be more than $7/8''$ to $1''$ wide when cut.

Lay one raw edge of bias along the seam edge, with right sides together (Fig. 84a). Stitch with a narrow seam allowance. Trim these edges to narrow, uniform width. Turn the bias over the raw edge of wool and turn under the other edge of bias so that the last folded edge meets the line of machine stitching (Fig. 84b). Hem this fold down by hand. Another way to finish the bias is to turn it over the raw edge, turn under the other edge of bias, and bring this last folded edge of bias down until it covers the line of machine stitching. Baste to position. You may now finish by machine instead of by hand. To do so, press the seam edges and the bias basted to them. Stitch, holding the right side of the wool fabric up. In this way, you can see and stitch in the groove formed by the first stitching which joined bias to wool edge. The stitching will catch the under fold of the bias.

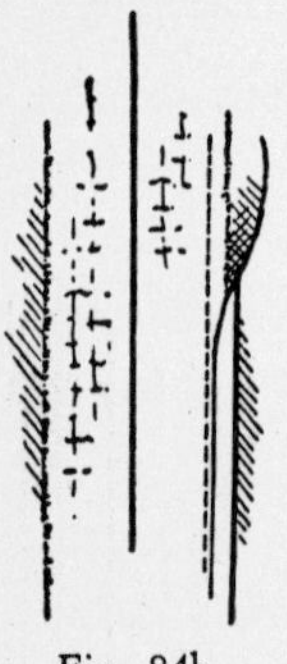

Fig. 84b

There is another satisfactory finish for fabrics that are not too bulky or stiff. Again, press the seam edges open. Turn under each raw edge about $1/8''$

and stitch this folded edge. Press again. Special care is needed with this finish to see that the edges of curved seams lie flat against the body of the jacket.

Where seam edges cannot be pressed open and have to be pressed together in one direction, it is wise to bind the two raw edges together. This is the usual treatment for the armscye seam. The edges of that seam naturally turn out into the sleeve. The seam edge on the sleeve, not on the jacket, should be shrunk during the pressing so that it is as flat and nonbulky as possible. The gathering threads used when the sleeve was set in may be used again to help shrink out the fullness. After this edge has been shrunk, the two edges of the seam may be bound together.

SHOULDER PADS

See directions, page 57.

Omit the "Basic Layer."

The so-called "Other Layers of Padding" are all that are used in an unlined jacket.

After pads are formed, cover both sides of each pad either with a piece of the wool fabric, if the wool is not bulky, or with a piece of lining fabric. This piece of fabric may be cut twice the size of the pad, so that one piece covers both sides of pad. Place it over the pad so that it is folded along a true bias line and so that this bias foldline lies along the edge of pad that will fall along armscye line.

Fig. 85a   Fig. 85b

If the pad is very thick along the edge across the top of shoulder, it may need an inset of the lining fabric (Fig. 85a). If so, cut two separate pieces of fabric, one for each side of the pad; cut a third piece for the inset.

Finish the edges around the inset smoothly by turning the raw edges toward each other and felling them together (Fig. 85b). The other edges may be finished with a binding; or the raw edges may be turned inside between the two layers and finished with a hand stitch such as overhanding. Edges should not be bulky or stiff lest they form a ridge under finished jacket.

UNDERCOLLAR, JOINING UNDERCOLLAR TO COAT, TOPCOLLAR

Previous directions under these topics may be followed with one exception: the raw edge of topcollar along the neckline should be finished neatly since there will be no lining to cover it. Sometimes this raw edge is covered with a bias tape laid flat over the seamline.

Stitch one edge of bias to the neckline of the wool collar. Press the seam edges toward the center of the bias. Hem the other edge of bias to the coat.

Sometimes there is a narrow fitted facing of wool across the back of the neck. If so, the two front facings may be stitched to the back-of-neck facing on the shoulder seamlines. The seams are pressed open (Fig. 86).

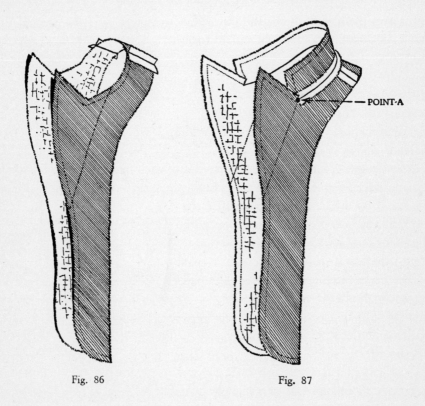

Fig. 86   Fig. 87

If the usual methods for custom tailoring have been followed up to this point, the front facings have been attached to the coat, the undercollar has been attached, and the topcollar has been attached. The next step, then, is to join the facings to the topcollar along the neckline. The simplest method is to turn under each edge of the neckline seam and join the folded edges with a fine, firm slip stitch.

Another method of treating both top- and undercollar and the front and back facings is indicated in Figures 86 through 89.

The two front facings are joined to the back facing on the shoulder seamlines. The seams are pressed open (Fig. 86). The topcollar is stitched to the front and back facings along the neckline seam. The seam is pressed open (Fig. 87). The undercollar is stitched to the coat along the neckline seam. The seam is pressed open (Fig. 88). These two portions (facings with topcollar and coat with undercollar) are laid together with right sides facing each other and with seamlines matched along front edges of coat and edges of collar. These outside edges are stitched together (Fig. 89). The seams are trimmed and graded, and the facings and collar are turned right side out.

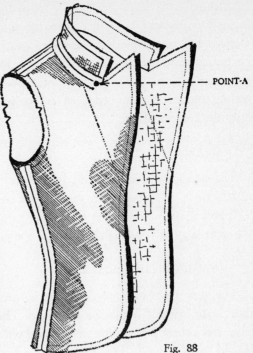

POINT·A

Fig. 88

There are three steps to be carefully handled with this method: (1) the point indicated by A in the Figures 87 and 88 should be exactly on the line of stitching and the two points A should exactly meet as shown by the A in Fig. 89; (2) when the facings and collars are turned right side out, the seam along the front edges and around the lapel should be rolled to the underside. Around the lapel, the term "rolled to the underside" means rolled toward the coat; along the

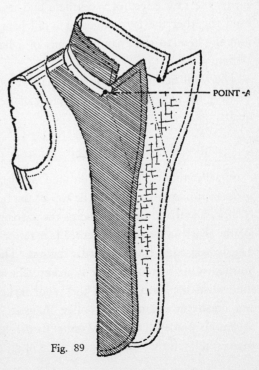

POINT -A

Fig. 89

front edges, the term means rolled toward the facing; (3) the topcollar, as always, should be larger than the undercollar. Up to this time, the method has not provided the extra size. Hold the collar folded on the creaseline, ease the topcollar fabric up from the neckline and down toward the outer edge of collar. Be sure the topcollar is eased enough to allow for rolling the outer seam edge of collar toward the undercollar. Baste to hold the ease in place.

SLEEVES

The design of sleeve should be simple. The one or two-piece sleeve is satisfactory. A sleeve with vent is not desirable. Previous directions for "Sleeves" page 76 may be followed. Finish the lower edge of sleeve in the same way as you finish the hem of the jacket.

HEMMING THE JACKET

The hem may be reinforced. If it is, previous directions for "Hemming the Coat," page 87 may be followed. There will be one point of difference: since there is no lining, the second way of finishing the top edge of hem should be followed. The method calls for the use of seam tape laid flat across the raw edges of wool hem and its reinforcement. It is possible to bind together the two edges of wool hem and its reinforcement and then join the hem to the coat by means of a hand stitch such as slip stitch or hemming.

The reinforcement of the hem may be omitted. The same directions for treating the hem may be used. Merely omit the parts that refer to reinforcement.

VARIATIONS OF UNLINED JACKET

A jacket that is otherwise unlined may have a piece of the wool fabric or a piece of lining fabric across the top of the back. This piece serves as a slight reinforcement and therefore helps the garment to hold its shape. (See Fig. 90 for the shape of this extra piece.) It is tailor basted to the back of the jacket. The lower edge line is usually bound. The armscye seam is stitched and finished with that of the wool jacket. The shoulder seamline may cover and thus finish the seam edge of the wool jacket. The neckline seam may cover and finish the seam of the collar. A usual way to treat the neckline seam when this piece is cut from wool is to stitch the topcollar to this facing in a plain seam and then to press the seam open.

Some European tailors use an interesting method of half-lining a jacket. The front is treated as a fully lined jacket except to cut the lining off just above or below the waistline. The lower edge of front lining is hemmed.

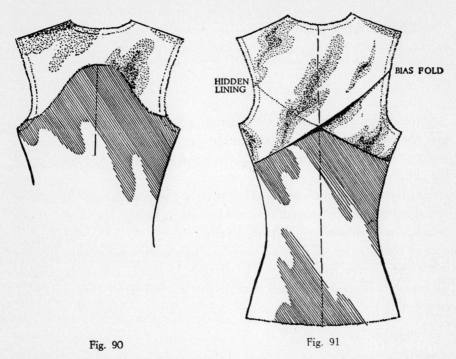

Fig. 90   Fig. 91

The wool seams which show below the lining are finished, as with a binding.

The back is half-lined with two bias pieces of lining fabric (Fig. 91).

CHILDREN'S COATS

If the design of coat is strictly tailored, whether it be for a boy or for a girl, the methods of making it are the same as for a custom-tailored coat for women. The directions previously given for such coats may then be used for the child's coat.

Usually the design chosen is not a strictly tailored one and the method of making is a combination of dressmaking and tailoring. The resulting coat is comparable to women's suits of the dressmaker type. The general difference in construction of the two types is that the dressmaker type has less reinforcement and less shaping. The design, the fabric, the reinforcement, the methods of construction all tend to give a softer result than they do in custom-tailored work.

TAPING

Read the directions for taping on page 23, and then note the points especially applicable to the child's coat as suggested below.

The armscye line should be taped. The back of neckline seam should be taped or a stay basting put in until the collar is attached. Few, if any, of the body seamlines need to be taped. They are so short that there will be little tendency for them to stretch during wear.

The method of applying tape is the same as above.

SHAPING COAT FRONT AND COAT BACK

See previous directions on pages 26–27. The only difference in shaping the child's coat is that there is less curve through the chest and bust, and none through the hip or waist area, except as provided by curved seams.

REINFORCEMENT

Wigan is a satisfactory type of reinforcement.

The reinforcement may be cut so as to reinforce shoulder, armscye, and front opening as in Fig. 92. Sometimes it is cut so as to reinforce only the front opening, as in Fig. 93. In either case, the shape is the same as the pattern of the coat, except at the inner edges. It has darts only where the coat has darts.

Stitching and shaping of reinforcement may follow previous directions, but there will be less shaping than with a woman's coat.

Attaching reinforcement to coat. See previous directions, page 45.

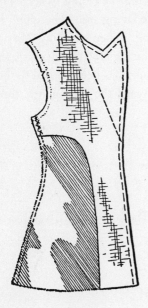 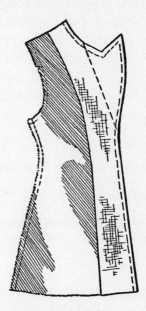

Fig. 92   Fig. 93

Design with notched lapel and collar. Padding may be entirely omitted, but it is wise to padstitch two rows on each side of creaseline of lapel, following previous directions page 47.

Creaseline of lapel and edges of front opening should be taped. (See page 48). Since lightweight reinforcement is being used, it may be trimmed away after the tape is applied, as previously suggested.

Design without lapel and with straight front opening. Padding and taping may be entirely omitted, or the edges of front opening only may be taped. If there is no taping, the reinforcement is held in place only by the stitching of the front edge seams. The two layers of wool and the one of reinforcement are attached together. The seam edge of reinforcement is cut away close to the stitching. If taping is omitted, the reinforcement is the only means by which edges are prevented from stretching. Fabrics which stretch readily should be taped.

FRONT FACING

Design with notched lapel. Follow previous directions, page 54.

All of this work may be done after the topcollar has been joined to the front facing. See directions below for topcollar.

Design without lapel. Such a design is usually for a coat that is to have a front opening from top to bottom and is not to lie half open as does a coat with a lapel as part of the design. In applying the facing to such a coat, the side to be eased is the coat side and not the facing side. Therefore, keep the coat side toward you as you apply the facing. When stitching, keep the coat side down against the feed dogs. After the facing is stitched, grade the seams so that the coat side is longer. After the facing has been turned to the wrong side of the coat, roll the seamline over toward the wrong side throughout the length of the front opening.

SEAMS

Treat as in previous directions, page 56.

SHOULDER PADS

Follow previous directions, page 57. The pad is usually softer, as well as smaller, than it is for women's coats.

UNDERCOLLAR

For the dressmaker type of coat, the preparation of this is different from that of the tailored coat collar.

The undercollar is usually of the same fabric as the coat. The undercollar and the reinforcement are cut from the same pattern and are identically alike. Tailor baste the two together lengthwise through the center. Tailor baste lengthwise near the outer edge and also near the neckline. In doing so, hold the collar curved as it will be on the finished coat. In this way the raw edges of the wool undercollar should slip outside of the raw edges of the rein forcement, so that the wool undercollar seems to be slightly larger than the reinforcement.

This undercollar may now be attached to the body of the coat throughout the length of the neckline of the collar. The seam is pressed open. The treat ment is described under "The Unlined Jacket" page 133 (Fig. 88).

TOPCOLLAR

The topcollar may be cut exactly the same size and shape as the under collar, or it may be cut ⅛″ larger all the way around. A finished topcollar always appears slightly smaller than it seemed to be at the time it was cut. The reason is that it must be made to curve over the undercollar with its reinforcement; also, the seam edge will be made to roll under toward the wrong side.

The topcollar may be joined to the front facing as far as the front facing extends along the neckline seam of the collar. The pattern used will indicate the relative position of the two. The seam is pressed open.

If a wool facing across back of neck is used, the facings of the two fronts and of the back are joined on the shoulder line as in Fig. 86. Then the top-collar is joined to front and back facing, as in Fig. 87.

JOINING FRONT FACING WITH TOPCOLLAR TO COAT WITH UNDER-COLLAR

Lay the right side of front facing and topcollar against the right side of coat and undercollar (Fig. 89). Hold the coat toward you while basting the edges of the front opening. If there is a lapel, hold the facing toward you while basting facing to the section that is to form the lapel. Hold the top-collar toward you while basting top- and undercollars together. Wherever you wish to conceal a seamline along an edge, hold toward you that side which will be rolled over the edge. Also, hold those same sides down against the feed dogs of the machine during stitching.

Grade the seam edges as usual. Trim away the seam edges of reinforcement. Turn the facing and collar right side out to its finished position.

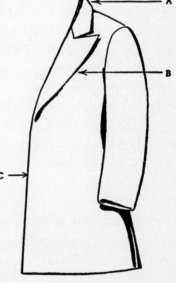

Roll the seamline along the edges, so that it will not show from the right side of the coat (Fig. 94). The seamline at the outer edge of the collar is rolled toward the undercollar (Fig. 94 point A). The seam-line around the lapel is rolled toward the coat, not toward the facing (Fig. 94 point B). It is rolled toward the facing along the front opening below the end of the lapel (Fig. 94, point C). If there is no lapel, it is rolled toward the facing throughout the length of the front opening.

Fig. 94

Catch together loosely the seam edges of the two seams along the gorgeline.

SLEEVES

Sleeves may be fitted and may be lined before they are stitched to the armscye of the coat, just as in women's coats. Or they may be fitted, shaped, and finished except for lining, and then stitched into the armscye. If the latter procedure is followed, it will mean that the sleeve lining will be attached after the sleeve is stitched into the coat.

HEMMING THE COAT

Follow previous directions, page 87.

LINING

Follow previous directions, page 97.

INTERLINING

Method 1 on page 103 is commonly used for children's coats, even though it results in a slightly bulkier garment than does the other method.

Special method for linings with or without interlining. After the body seams of the lining have been stitched and pressed, lay the right side of the lining against the right side of the body of the coat, carefully adjusting the one to the other, so that the finished lining will be in correct position. Bring the front facings into such a position that you can pin, baste, and stitch the free edge of wool front facing to the corresponding edge of lining. Turn the lining and coat into their finished position with the lining against the wrong side of the coat. The shoulder seams, neckline seam, armscye seam may be finished by hand as in previous directions. Also, the armscye seamline of the sleeve may be finished as in previous directions.

PRESSING

Previous directions for pressing may be used. See pages 106.

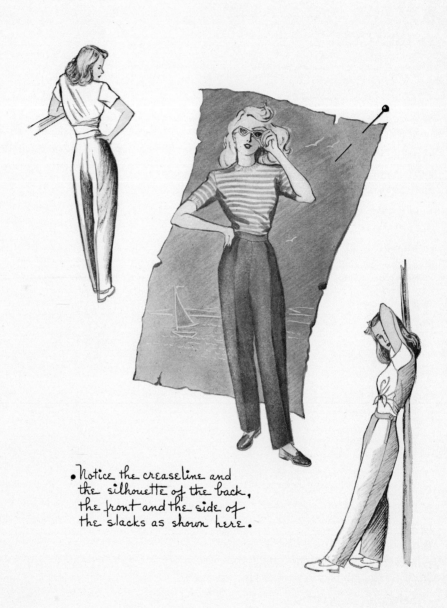

Notice the creaseline and
the silhouette of the back,
the front and the side of
the slacks as shown here.

SLACKS

Slacks require as much care and precision in their construction as does a custom-tailored coat. Precision is the essential quality. It is dependent on correct procedure from the time of selecting pattern and fabric to that of the final pressing.

Fitting seems to be the most difficult process, perhaps because the worker does not know how to apply basic principles of fitting to this garment. The result should give a trim neat effect, not only through the waistline and hip areas, but through the crotch and thigh areas.

The surface of the garment should have a flat effect which results from correctly executed construction processes, correct order of procedure in putting the garment together, and correct pressing. It is important to "press as you go," so that the final pressing is merely a light finish.

Pressing follows the usual methods, in order to give flat, smooth results. There is little shaping to be done. The final pressing adds the creaseline to the legs. The placement of this line is a "make or mar" process. "Well fitted and trim" suggest good-looking slacks.

PATTERN SELECTION

Select the pattern according to hip measure. If the size of hip is correct, it is easy to fit to a smaller or larger waistline. If the thigh is larger than usual, it may be necessary to use a pattern that is one size larger than the hip measure indicates is needed. It is difficult to let out the legs through the thigh area; but if the slacks are large enough there, it is easy to fit them in to a relatively smaller hipline. Sometimes, the sole cause of dissatisfaction with slacks is insufficient ease through the thigh.

Selection of pattern may be made according to the position of placket opening and to the type of pockets desired.

PATTERN TESTING AND ALTERATION

Measurements. Measure the body for size of waist, hip, and thigh; total

141

length of crotch; and length at the side from waistline to the lower edge of leg of slacks. Measure the pattern along corresponding lines.

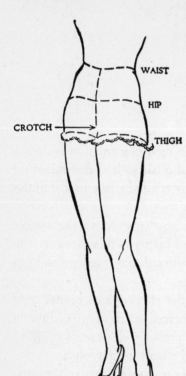

Fig. 95

The crotch measurement is taken on the body from the waistline in the center back down through the crotch and up to the waistline in the center front. The measuring tape should be drawn close to the body, though not tightly so. The thigh measurement is taken around the leg where the thigh is largest. This line is usually an inch or more below the lowest part of the crotch.

Check each body measurement against each pattern measurement to see that the pattern allows enough ease in each case. Allowances for ease are suggested below, with illustration of body and pattern measurement in Figs. 95, 96.

After checking the measurements in this way, pin the pattern pieces together, pin in darts also, and test the pattern by holding it against the body. There is danger of tearing the pattern in this process, so it may be wise to pin darts and inside leg seam only. Place the pattern with the pinned leg seam against the inside of the leg; bring it into position at crotch and waistline; at center front and back, pin to a tape around waistline; bring the other edges of pattern to the side of body and adjust them on the line from waistline to ankle.

Neither of these two methods of pattern testing is entirely reliable, if used alone. When both are used, the one tends to verify the findings of the other.

Alterations. No changes should be necessary in the circumference of the leg from thighline down to hem. Changes in size of hip may be made by taking in or letting out the seamlines of the outside leg seam. This is usually a straight or nearly straight line. Changing it will entail two other changes. The pattern markings for side placket openings and for side pockets should be placed along the new seam line. The size of waistline will have been changed and this should be corrected by taking in or letting out the darts. Note that the seamlines of crotch are not altered.

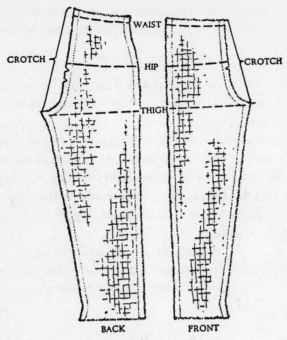

Fig. 96

BODY AND PATTERN MEASUREMENTS

Body Measurement		Allowance for Ease	Pattern Measurement
Waistline	28″	1″	29″
Hipline	37″	4″ or more	41″ or more
Thighline (each leg)	19″	2″ or more	21″ or more
Crotchline	24″	5″	29″
Length from waist to hem	43″	½″	43½″

Changes in length should be made between the thighline and hemline, or between the hipline and waistline. The latter change alters length of crotchline. Pattern instruction sheets show these changes clearly.

Previous directions for pattern layout, pattern cutting, and pattern marking, as well as for fabric design in layout and cutting may be followed. (See pages 13–17.)

FABRIC SELECTION

If the slacks are to be made of wool, the fabric should be of a firm, close weave so that they may be well tailored and pressed and will hold their shape during wear. Since there will be little shaping done by means of pressing, the fabric does not need to have the pliability and sponginess that are helpful in the making of a coat.

Fabrics other than wool should have the same general characteristics of firmness and closeness of weave. Wrinkle-resistant finishes are desirable.

PREPARATION OF FABRIC AND OTHER SUPPLIES

Wool fabrics should be sponged and shrunk, and grainlines should be straightened and marked as suggested under "Preparation of Wool Fabrics and Other Supplies," page 6.

Other fabrics should be shrunk as with any cotton or rayon fabric for other garments. Ironing which follows shrinking should be done lengthwise of the warp grainlines first. Then give a light finish by ironing crosswise or fillingwise. During this ironing, grainlines should be watched so that filling lines are always at right angles to warplines.

Reinforcement fabrics and fabrics used for placket facings or pocket linings should be thoroughly shrunk and ironed.

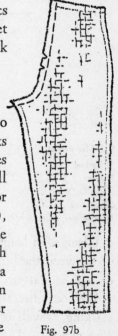

ORDER OF PROCEDURE

There is a choice between two orders of procedure in putting slacks together. Briefly, the difference lies between (1) making crotch and all leg seams before the side pocket or placket opening is made, and (2), making the outside leg seams and the pocket and placket before the crotch and inside leg seams are finished. It is a little easier to handle the construction of the pocket and placket in the latter method, for the slacks may still be laid out flat on the table while the

Fig. 97a   Fig. 97b

pocket is made. On the other hand, it may be easier to understand the processes of making the pocket if the seams are made first. The order suggested here follows the first, namely, finishing crotch and inner and outer leg seams before making pockets and placket.

Preparation for first fitting. Baste darts in front and in back.

Baste center front seam of crotch (Fig. 97a).

Baste center back seam of crotch (Fig. 97b).

Baste each inner leg seam beginning at the crotch.

Baste the outer leg seams, leaving the usual opening at top of left-hand side for the placket opening; on both sides, if there are two openings. If there is a center front closing, leave the front crotch seam open part way.

Baste or pin the belt to the top of slacks. This may seem to be an un-necessary step, but it is not. The fabric may stretch during fitting, and the slacks will drop below the waistline so that hip and crotchlines are not in correct position. Mark the line of the side opening on the back edge and on front edge, or on each side of the center front opening.

First fitting. Check first through hip- and thighlines, to see that slacks are in position there, and that there is sufficient ease. This step includes checking size and fit through the area of the buttocks.

Check through waistline.

Check total length.

Procedure after first fitting. Stitch, finish, and press darts.

Stitch, finish, and press crotch seams.

Stitch, finish, and press inner leg seams.

Stitch, finish, and press outer leg seams.

Make placket and pockets.

Sew on fasteners for placket. Press.

If necessary, try on again.

Attach belt or other finish of waistline. Sew on fasteners. Press.

Second fitting. Check lower hemline.

Procedure after second fitting. Finish hemline. Press.

Final pressing. The slacks should need only a light pressing, except for the creaselines.

CUTTING AND MARKING

Previous directions for cutting and marking for the tailored coat on page 14 may be followed. Whether the slacks are to be of wool or of other fabric, the same principles apply to cutting and marking.

CONSTRUCTION

Darts. See "Treatment of Darts" page 25.

Some darts, especially the ones in the front, are combinations of darts and tucks, so that they do not have a pointed end. There is a fold, like that at the end of a tuck. The stitching line may follow the line indicated by the pattern and then follow a line across the end of the dart (Fig. 98) or merely double back on the first line.

Crotch seams. Three factors determine the choice of type of seam. They are the effect desired for the outside of the slacks, the fact that the seam is curved, and the fact that the seam is subjected to much strain while the slacks are being worn.

Desirable effects are flatness and simplicity. A plain seam with edges pressed open results in these qualities. It is satisfactory, too, for the curve of the seam line. It is not particularly strong, however. The finish of the edges may add to the strength. Edge finishes may be:

Fig. 98

Pinking.

Overcasting.

Raw edges turned under $\frac{1}{8}''$ and stitched. (This finish is difficult to handle on the deepest part of the curve.)

Binding.

Surface stitching $\frac{1}{8}''$ from the line of the first stitching, and along each side of it.

A welt seam is strong, though not so flat as a plain seam. To make it, stitch as for a plain seam. Grade the edges so that the longer seam edge will lie next to the outside of the garment. Press both edges in the direction planned. Surface stitch along a line that follows the first stitching line, but $\frac{1}{8}''$ to $\frac{1}{4}''$ away from it. When this seam is used, be sure that the crotch seam of the back and that of the front are finished so that the edges are pressed in the same direction on the two sections of the crotch.

A 3" or 4" strip of narrow tape may be stitched to the seam along its deepest curve. It is joined to the seam either when the seam is being stitched or after the seam is finished.

Inner leg seams. The choice of type of finish may be the same as for crotch seams, even though this seam is not so curved. A welt seam is not often used here.

Special care is needed where the leg seams cross the crotch seams, for there is much bulk of fabric and there will be much strain along this line. First, be sure that the free edges of the crotch seams lie flat against the surface layer of fabric. See that corresponding lines of stitching of the two leg seams and of the two crotch seams meet as they should. After the first stitching of the leg seams, some of the fabric of the seam edges may be cut away where there is the greatest bulk. The trimming must be carefully done, lest the seam be weakened. Then a narrow tape may be stitched to one of the two seams, the leg, or the crotch seam. It usually lies along the leg seam and crosses the crotch seam. The tape is only 3″ or 4″ long. It is stitched to the seam, even if the

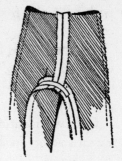

Fig. 99

seam finish does not have a surface stitching. It may be put in by hand so that no stitching shows on the right side (Fig. 99).

Outer leg seams. The effect desired is the chief basis for choice of type of seam here. The usual choices are plain seams with edges pressed open, or welt seams. If a welt seam is used, the edges on the wrong side of the slacks should be turned, pressed, and stitched toward the front of the garment. By turning them toward the front, the seam, the placket, and the pocket finish will have an unbroken line, so far as outside appearance is concerned.

Pockets and plackets. Directions for pockets and placket openings are such that different combinations may be used according to design of slacks desired. For example, with these directions the slacks may have:

1. A left side placket opening, and a right side pocket.
2. Two side pockets and a fly front opening.
3. A pocket-placket combination on right and left side each.

To simplify directions for pockets, they all indicate that the pocket extends from the waistline downward. This is the case when the slacks are finished with a belt. The belt holds the top of pocket in place. When the waistline is finished with a facing, the lower line of facing holds the top of pocket in place. The outer edge of placket opening at the top which is not finished with the pocket pieces is finished with the facing.

Side pocket set in a seam. This pocket is simple to make, if the general idea of the finished product is clear to the worker. It is like a bag, the open top of which is formed by the two sides of the opening left at the top of the side seamline.

When using cotton or rayon for the slacks, the several pieces may be cut from the same fabric as that for the slacks. There is no need for an extra piece of facing. When using wool, the pocket facings are cut of wool and the pocket linings from silesia or lining fabric, if the latter is durable enough.

Cut two strips for pocket facings from wool. Cut them lengthwise of the warp and 2½'' wide. The length is 1'' longer than the length of the pocket opening. Mark on each the point which indicates the end of the pocket opening.

Cut two identical pieces for the pocket linings. Commercial patterns are satisfactory in shape and size. One edge of pocket lining is cut with the same degree of curve and on the same grain as the front edge of the side opening. The length of this line is equal to the length of the pocket opening plus 3'' to 5''. This edge will be joined to the front edge of the opening. The top edge of lining is 2½'' to 3'' wide. This will be joined to the waistline seam or facing. The other edge is curved so that the widest section is 2'' or 3'' below the point which marks the end of the pocket opening. The two long curved edges of the two pieces of the pocket lining will be joined together, but they will not be joined to the slacks (Fig. 100a).

Mark accurately the point which indicates the end of the pocket opening, Point A, Fig. 100a.

On the slacks and on the pocket pieces, check the length of all four edges (six edges when facings of wool are used), and see that all pieces are marked accurately so as to indicate the length from the top of pocket to the lower point of the pocket opening. The length is about 7''. To simplify directions, this marked point will be indicated again as point A.

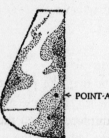

← POINT·A

Fig. 100a

Lay the wool facing, right side up, against the right side of the lining piece, with straight edges matched and with points A matched. Only the inner and lower edges are now joined to the pocket

A

Fig. 100b

lining. These two edges may be closely zigzag stitched to the lining or they may be turned under and surface stitched to the lining (Fig. 100b). Face both pieces of pocket lining in this way. From this point on, there is no difference between the method of making the pocket when the slacks are of wool, and when they are of other fabric.

Lay the edge of lining with the facing attached against the back edge of the opening left in seamline of slacks. Match raw edges and points A. Right sides of fabric face each other. Stitch this line (Fig. 100c). **Turn** all raw edges on the wrong side toward the back. Turn the lining toward the front. Fig. 100g shows direction of seam edges and of pocket linings. Grade the seam edges. Press. Depending upon the way in which the outer leg seam was finished on the wrong side, the seam edge may or may not need to be clipped to point A, in order to allow the seam edge above point A to turn toward the back.

Seam the second piece of the lining to the front edge of opening in the same way. Turn the seam edges and the pocket lining toward the front. Fig. 100d shows the lining attached, seam edges correctly turned, and the lining ready to be turned back toward the front. Grade the seam edges. Press. Surface stitch ⅛″ to ¼″ from the folded edge, from

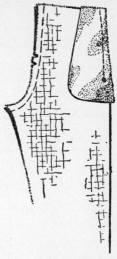

Fig. 100c

point A to a point that is 1″ to 1½″ below the top edge of the slacks (Fig. 100e).

Put the pocket into its closed position, as it will be when the slacks are worn. The edge lines of the pocket should be in line with the seam below the pocket. Hold it closed by basting (Fig. 100f).

Now complete the line of surface stitching along the edge of the front side of pocket. This

Fig. 100d

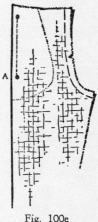

Fig. 100e

is the 1″ to 1½″ at the top previously left unstitched (Fig. 100f). In this way, the front side of pocket is stitched down to the back side of pocket.

Turn garment to the wrong side. The two pieces of pocket lining are lying together with edges matched. If work was inaccurate, the edges may need to be trimmed until they are matched. Baste and stitch the edges from point A down along the straight edge and up around the curved edge (Fig. 100g). These seam edges should be finished so as to be durable and nonfraying.

Bar tacks may be worked across the upper and lower ends of pocket open-

ing just where the first line of surface stitching began and ended. Bar tacks
add to strength of pocket opening and give a tailored effect.

Side placket openings. These may be finished with fabric and fasteners such
as buttons and buttonholes, or with slide fasteners. Directions for each are
given here.

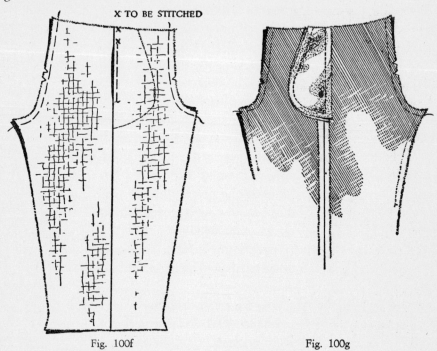

Fig. 100f   Fig. 100g

Bound and faced placket (modified). Only one method of making this placket
is suggested. It is a quick method, easy to understand and to make, and it

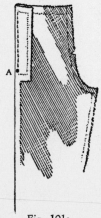

Fig. 101a

gives flat, durable results. It may be fastened with
hooks and eyes, snap fasteners, or with buttons and
buttonholes.

Point A will again be the means of designating the
point at the lower end of the opening.

Cut one strip of fabric lengthwise of the warp grain
about 1⅜″ wide and as long as the opening plus 1″.
This strip should be wide enough to provide for buttonholes, if they are to be used. To determine the width in
this case, decide on length of buttonholes, then add at
least ½″ and two seam allowances. This piece is to be
the facing for the front or upper lap of placket.

Cut another strip of fabric, also lengthwise of warp

grain, and also as long as the opening plus 1″ and about 2¼″ wide. This piece is to form the back or under lap of placket.

Face the front edge of the opening with the narrower strip. Let the 1″ of extra length of facing fall below point A (Fig. 101a). Depending on the firmness of fabric used for the slacks, it may or may not be wise to lay a strip of reinforcement fabric (thin but firm) between the facing and the slacks. If reinforcement is used, cut it the same size and shape as the facing, minus the seam allowances. Lay it inside the seam allowances of the facing and tailor baste it into position (Fig. 101b). If the slacks are of wool, it is reasonable to face this edge with firm lining fabric. After the edge is stitched and the facing turned to wrong side, surface stitch the folded edge. This folded edge should begin at point A and thus be in line with the seam-line, but the surface stitching is just inside the folded edge.

Turn under the inside edge of facing against itself and edge-stitch. This inside edge of the facing need not be sewed down to the body of the slacks when buttonholes are to be used, for they will hold it in place. If snap fasteners are to be used, they

Fig. 101b

may be sewed onto the facing before this inner edge is sewed down. It may be sewed down by hand or by machine, but this is done later. See below.

Fold the wider strip down the center lengthwise and press.

Turn under the seam allowance on the back edge of the opening ⅛″ outside of seamline. Lay this folded edge over the raw edges of the folded strip, working from the right side of slacks. Surface stitch the two together. These three raw edges on the wrong side should be overcast (Fig. 101c).

Pin the placket into its closed position, as it will be when worn. Turn slacks to the wrong side. See that the facing strip on the front edge and the doubled strip on the back edge are matched. Pin together the ends of these two strips, which are loose below point A. Stitch them together from side to side in a slight upward

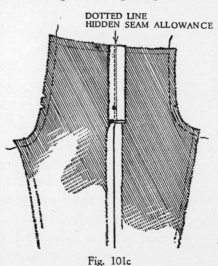

DOTTED LINE
HIDDEN SEAM ALLOWANCE

Fig. 101c

slant from point A. The slanting line of stitching protects the seamline from undue strain. The raw edges at the end may be trimmed and overcast (Fig. 101d).

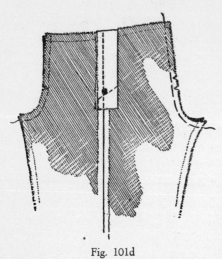

From the right side, stitch across the lower end of placket, or work a short bartack at the lower end, while the placket is still pinned in its closed position.

Now is the time to sew the inner edge of the facing on the front side of opening to the slacks, if this edge is not to be left loose. Remove the pins and open the placket and stitch along inner edge of facing. See that this stitching exactly meets the surface stitching across the lower end, if that line was machine stitched.

Fig. 101d

Note that several stitchings begin or end, or pass through point A. It is especially at this point that care should be taken to see that the placket is strong and also flat.

Fig. 101e shows a finished placket of this type.

Side placket opening with zipper. The side opening should be ½″ longer than the metal part of the zipper. This half inch provides for ¼″ above the

POINT-A

Fig. 101e

zipper catch and ¼″ below the metal stop. The two allowances mean that the zipper, instead of the fabric, receives the strain of use.

The front edge of the opening is faced with a strip of fabric 1¼″ wide and 1″ longer than the opening. This is cut on the warp grain, if the line of the opening is straight; or a long bias if the line is curved. If the slacks are wool, the facing may be made of lining fabric. When turning the facing to the wrong side of opening, roll the seam slightly under the folded edge so that the facing does not show from the right side. The extra length of the facing strip lies free below the lower end of the opening. Be sure that the folded edge forms a continuous line with the seamline below the opening. Press the faced edge.

If the slacks fabric is firm and if there is an extra width (at least 1″) of seam allowance on the opening, this front edge need not be faced; the seam allowance may be turned back in line with the seamline below the opening. Since this folded edge may stretch, a strip of reinforcement fabric cut lengthwise of the warp grain and 1″ wide may be laid under the hem. The raw edge of the reinforcement may be stitched to a single thickness of the fabric before the hem is turned. The stitching line should lie just under the folded edge of the opening after the hem is turned back.

Whether facing or hem is to be used, turn the slacks wrong side out and baste together in a plain seam the front and back edges of the opening, exactly in line with the seamline below the opening. This basting simplifies and ensures accuracy in the remaining processes.

With the wrong side toward you, crease the seam allowance of the back side of the opening, ⅛″ from the basted seamline and parallel to it. The seam edge still turns toward the back of the slacks. Baste.

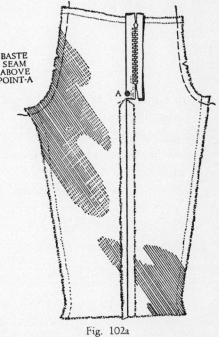

BASTE
SEAM
ABOVE
POINT·A

Fig. 102a

Keep the zipper closed throughout the following work. Lay the zipper under this ⅛″ tuck, so that right side of tuck and right side of zipper are placed as they will be when in use on the finished garment. Check the position carefully (Fig. 102a).

Tuck is ⅛″ away from the metal portion. The metal stop at the lower end of the zipper is ¼″ above the lower end of the opening. The upper end of the metal is ¼″ or more below the raw edge of top of opening. Baste and stitch close to the edge of the tuck and through tuck and zipper tape only.

Bring the zipper into position as it is to be when the slacks are being worn. This motion will bring the other edge of the zipper tape against the facing or hem of the front edge of the opening (Fig. 102a). Baste lengthwise through the facing or hem and the zipper tape. From the right side, stitch this line so as to provide room for the zipper pull. A reasonable space and line is ½″ away from opening and parallel to it. Across the lower end, stitch in a downward slant just below the metal of the zipper (Fig.

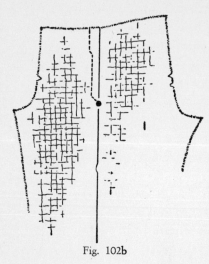

Fig. 102b

102b). Remove the bastings that hold the opening in a closed position.

Depending on the type of seam and seam finish used in the outer leg seam below the opening, the seam edge may need to be clipped just below point A, so that the 1/8" tuck and the seam edge will lie flat (Fig. 102a). or the folded edge of tuck below the opening may be gradually unfolded until it runs into the seam edge. If this treatment is used, the new line needs firm pressing. The raw edges along the opening may be trimmed to a line close to the edges of zipper tape and the edges may be overcast together.

If a lingerie guard is desired, cut a strip of fabric warpwise, 2" wide and 1" longer than the opening. Fold it double lengthwise and press. After the 1/8" tuck has been formed along the back side of the opening and after the zipper has been laid under the tuck, lay this guard under the zipper, with the folded edge extending toward the front. The stitching then passes through the tuck, zipper tape, and guard.

Waistline finishes. The pattern for slacks will provide for a top facing or a band. When a facing is planned, the body of the slacks is cut higher than it is when a band is to be used. This additional length is slightly shaped to fit the curve of the waistline.

Facing finish. Cut a strip of true bias from slacks fabric about 2" wide and long enough for the waistline plus seam or end finishes. If the slacks are of wool, this strip may be cut of lining fabric. Also, this facing may be a fitted one instead of a bias one.

Cut a strip of true bias from reinforcement fabric such as wigan or muslin. The width is the same as the facing minus one seam allowance. The length is the same as the facing minus seam allowances.

Lay the reinforcement against the wrong side of the facing and with the one seam allowance of facing extending beyond the reinforcement. Tailor baste the two together through the center lengthwise. Turn the one seam allowance of the facing over the edge of the reinforcement and baste. Press this edge. This edge will be the lower line when the facing has been joined to the slacks.

Place the other edge of facing against the top of the slacks, right sides together and raw edges coinciding. Stitch this top line through slacks, facing, and reinforcement. Trim away seam edge of reinforcement as closely as possible. Grade the other two seam edges.

Turn facing to wrong side of slacks. Roll the seam over to the wrong side so that it is $\frac{1}{8}''$ from the top edge. Baste. Press lightly.

Trim the reinforcement in line with the finished ends of facing, if further trimming is necessary.

Turn the ends of the facing over the ends of the reinforcement and against placket openings, so that the folded ends of facing lie just inside the outer edge of placket.

Baste the lower edge of facing into position against the slacks. The edge has already been turned over the reinforcement and basted. This edge will lap over the upper edges of pocket linings and will hold them in place.

The facing may now be surface stitched across the top and lower edges and across the ends. Or the top and lower edges of facing may be surface stitched and the ends finished by hand.

Belt finish. Cut a strip of fabric lengthwise with the warp grain. Use the same fabric as for the slacks. The width is equal to the width of belt desired, plus two seam allowances. Note that "top of slacks" includes the extra length due to the lap of the placket opening.

Cut a strip of reinforcement fabric on the true bias and of the same length and width as the belt, but without any seam allowance.

Place the reinforcement strip against the wrong side of belt fabric so that seam allowances of belt extend beyond the reinforcement on each side and each end. Tailor baste into position lengthwise through the center.

Turn one long edge and both ends of belt over the edges of reinforcement and catstitch the edges to the reinforcement (Fig. 103a). These stitches do not pass through to the right side of belt. Press.

Lay the other long edge of belt against the top edge of slacks, right sides together. Baste and stitch the seamline (Fig. 103a). Grade the seam edges and turn them upward onto the belt. Press.

The belt is now ready to face. The facing may be cut from the slacks fabric if it is cotton or rayon, or it may be cut from lining fabric if the slacks

Fig. 103a

fabric is wool. Cut the facing strip lengthwise of the warp and of the same size and shape as the belt was cut.

Each long edge and each end of facing may be turned under and pressed and then the facing may be placed against the wrong side of the belt. The folded edge of facing should fall inside of the folded edges of belt by ⅛″ or less. At least, it should not show from the right side of belt. Tailor baste facing into position against belt. Hem the edges of facing to the belt (Figs. 103b and 104).

Instead of turning the top edge of belt over the reinforcement and cat-stitching the raw edge to the reinforcement, the belt may be faced in exactly

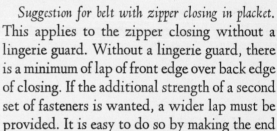

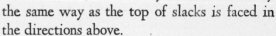

the same way as the top of slacks is faced in the directions above.

Suggestion for belt with zipper closing in placket. This applies to the zipper closing without a lingerie guard. Without a lingerie guard, there is a minimum of lap of front edge over back edge of closing. If the additional strength of a second set of fasteners is wanted, a wider lap must be provided. It is easy to do so by making the end

Fig. 103b

of the belt on the back side of the closing 1″ or more longer than the top of the slacks. This extra length is finished with the belt and merely extends beyond the edge of the back side of the closing and provides a place for the second set of fasteners (Fig. 104).

Buttonholes. If there is to be a buttonhole, either worked or bound, at the end of the belt, the bias reinforcement should be cut away from the area of the buttonhole and replaced by a piece of reinforcement fabric cut so that the warpline will run in the same direction as the buttonhole.

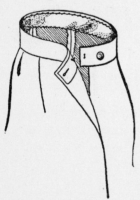

If the buttonhole is to be of the bound type, it is made in the outside layer of the belt before the belt is joined to the slacks. The wrong side is finished after the facing is joined to the belt. Bound buttonholes are not usually as satisfactory in slacks as are the worked ones.

Worked buttonholes are made after the belt is joined to the slacks and after the belt is faced and entirely finished. A tailored eyelet buttonhole is strong and adds to the tailored effect of the gar-ment.

Fig. 104

In addition to a button closing, it is often wise to have hooks and eyes for added strength. Hooks and eyes may be used where the finish of the side opening has left the front edge lapped over the back edge, as with the faced and bound placket or with the zipper closing with lingerie guard. The eyes are sewed onto the end of the back side of the belt. The location of the hooks depends on the width of the lap at ends of belt (Fig. 104).

The zipper closing without lingerie guard provides a minimum of lap, just enough for hooks and eyes close to the two ends, unless the suggestion above for adding length to belt has been carried out. (See "Suggestion for Belt with Zipper Closing in Placket," page 156.)

Finish for lower line of legs. The pattern usually provides for a hem finish. Turn allowance for hem onto wrong side. Baste the foldline and press lightly. See that the hem fits the body of the leg. If either leg seam should be slanted even a little, the allowance for the hem must be slanted an equal amount and in the same direction (Fig. 105).

The hem may be reinforced just as the hem of a coat is reinforced. (See page 87.)

The upper edge of hem may be turned under and stitched and this folded edge may then be slipstitched to the body of the leg. Or the raw edge may be bound and the binding slipstitched to the body of the leg. A straight or bias seam tape may finish the raw edge of the hem. The upper edge of tape is slipstitched to the body of leg.

Fly front closing with zipper. Since fly fronts are usually finished with zippers, these directions are for that type only. This particular closing is a phase of the fashion for the mannish in women's clothing. For that reason, the directions here are for an opening that fastens toward the

Fig. 105

right instead of toward the left. Women's clothes usually fasten toward the left. Directions may be reversed easily, if desired.

The crotch seam is finished to point A, which designates the point at which the seamline ends and the opening begins.

To face the upper lap or left edge of opening, cut a strip from fabric of slacks 2" wide and as long as the opening plus 1". This facing strip may be lengthwise of the warp grain.

If the grain line of the edge of opening in slacks is quite slanted, it may be preferable to cut this strip on a long or garment bias. Such a bias is slanted a little away from the warpline.

Lay this strip against the upper or left edge of opening, right sides together and with the 1" extra length extending below point A. Stitch

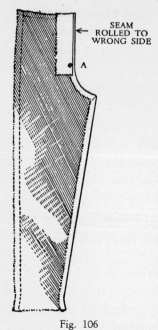

SEAM
← ROLLED TO
WRONG SIDE

• A

Fig. 106

facing strip to slacks from point A upward and just outside of the seamline which lies below point A. "Just outside" should be less than ⅛". Turn the facing to the wrong side and roll the seamline slightly toward the wrong side. The outside folded edge of the opening is in line with the seamline below point A, but the facing does not show at this edge (Fig. 106). Edge-stitch the loose inner edge of facing and overcast the raw edge. Do not sew this edge down to the body of the slacks (Fig. 106). Turn slacks to the wrong side and baste the two edges of the opening together in a plain seam exactly in line with the seam stitching below point A.

On the right-hand side of opening, fold the seam allowance ⅛" away from the basting on the seamline and parallel to it. Work with zipper closed during the next steps. Lay the zipper under this folded edge so that outside of slacks and outside of zipper are matched. Fig. 107 shows how this step would appear if the placket edges had not been basted together. Since

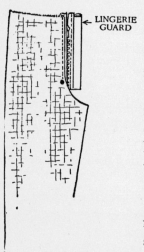

← LINGERIE
GUARD

Fig. 107

you are working from the wrong side of slacks, you may mistakenly put the zipper in wrong side out, so that it would be unusable on the finished garment. Place edge of tuck ⅛" away from metal teeth of zipper. See that metal stop at lower end of zipper is ¼" above point A and that there is ¼" extension of opening above the metal of the zipper. Baste tuck to zipper tape. This process is identical with that in the side placket with zipper closing (Fig. 102a).

To make a lingerie guard, cut a strip of slacks fabric lengthwise of the warp, 2" wide and as long as the opening, plus 1". Fold lengthwise through the center and press. If the slacks are of wool, the guard may be cut single width from wool and then faced with lining fabric. If this is done, be sure that the wool side is toward the outside of the slacks when the guard is joined to the opening.

Place the guard under the zipper so that the zipper lies between the slacks and the guard, and so that the folded edge of guard extends beyond the tape of zipper and toward the edge of the opening (Fig. 107).

Stitch close to edge of tuck through slacks, zipper tape and guard (Fig. 107).

Now fold the body of the slacks and the guard out of the way. Baste the other edge of the zipper tape to the front facing, which has been left loose. Do not baste through to the surface of the slacks. At this point, it is wise to turn the slacks right side out and make sure that each step has been correctly and accurately executed. Slacks, facing, zipper, and guard should lie flat and smooth. You cannot test the zipper by opening it, because the basting still holds the opening together.

Again from the wrong side, stitch zipper tape to the facing only, in a line $\frac{1}{8}''$ from the metal of the zipper. The edge of facing will extend beyond the tape.

Lay the facing in place against the body of the slacks. Baste. Turn the slacks right side out and stitch through slacks and facing. This line of stitching does not pass through zipper tape. The stitching is $1\frac{1}{4}''$ or more away from the outer, folded edge of the upper lap. It is parallel to this edge except toward the lower end where it curves toward the outer edge and ends at point A.

Pocket and placket in a side opening. Only one method is suggested here. There are several ways of making the pocket-placket combination, each yielding results slightly different from the others. If one method has been successfully followed, commercial pattern directions for the others are easily understood and carried out. Or it is easy to copy a type that has been observed in another garment.

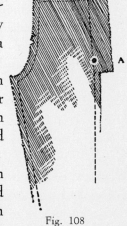

Fig. 108

This method may be used only where there is an outer leg seam in which an opening is left in the upper end. The point at which the stitching of the leg seam ends and at which the opening begins is designated as point A.

It is helpful if the back side of the opening has been cut with an extension sufficient to provide a hemmed underlap of the placket. The width of the extension should be $2\frac{1}{2}''$ wide and should extend from the top of slacks to a point 1'' below point A (Fig. 108). Turn the extension back onto the wrong side of slacks to form a hem. The first fold of the hem should be in line with the seamline below point A. The outer folded edge extends beyond the seamline by more than an inch. Slipstitch the hem to the slacks. If the fabric is not firm, this hem should be reinforced by a piece of reinforcement fabric. The fasteners used for the closing will be sewed to this extension hem. To reinforce, cut a strip of fabric the same size and shape as the finished hem. This strip has no seam allowances. Lay it inside the hem and turn the hem over it.

If the back has not been cut with an extension sufficient for underlap and hem, the extension provided may be faced; or if it is too narrow even for an underlap, the back edge of the opening will have to be bound. In either case,

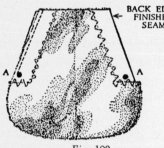

BACK EDGE
← FINISHED
    SEAM

Fig. 109

there must be an extension to provide an underlap, and this underlap must be double and must have finished edges.

Cut a piece of fabric for the pocket lining. The fabric should be firm and strong but not bulky. The size varies, but is 7″ to 10″ wide at the top and 11″ long. It is cut lengthwise of the warp grain through the center. The slant of the sides is the same degree of slant as the edges of the opening above the leg seam. The length of the sides is equal to the length of the placket opening plus 4″ or 5″ (Fig. 109).

Cut two strips for facing the sides of the pocket linings. Use the slacks fabric, cut lengthwise of the warp grain, and make each strip 2″ wide and as long as the opening plus 1″.

One strip is stitched to the back edge of the pocket lining to form a facing. The facing is turned onto the right side of the lining. The seam edge is rolled toward the lining side so that the lining does not show along the edge. Turn the inside edge and lower end of facing against the lining and surface stitch. In wool, these edges may be left raw, edgestitched and zigzagged. Leave top end unfinished (Fig. 109).

The other strip is joined to the front edge of pocket lining in a different way. Lay it right side up, against the right side of lining. Match the raw edges and edgestitch. Treat the inside edge and lower end of facing as in facing the back edge of pocket lining. The difference between facings on front and back edge of pocket lining is that the outer edge of the back is finished with a seam but the outer edge of the front has surface stitching close to raw edges (Fig. 109).

If a button closing is to be used, buttonholes may be made now through the facing and lining. Be sure they are made in the back edge of pocket lining.

This back edge of pocket lining serves as upper lap of placket also.

With slacks and pocket lining right side up, lay the back edge of the pocket lining on top of the back edge of the opening which is already hemmed, faced, or bound. The finished edge of the pocket lining lies just outside of the seamline in the leg seam. "Outside," as usual, means nearer the raw edge of the seam. The distance is less than $\frac{1}{4}''$. To ensure accuracy,

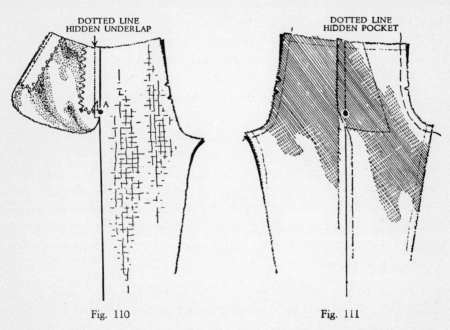

Fig. 110   Fig. 111

this back edge of pocket lining may be basted to the back edge of the opening throughout its length. But only one small section is machine stitched. Stitch 1″ only along the faced edge from 1″ above point A to point A. Then stitch across the end of the facing. This 1″ and the distance across the end are the only places in which the back edge of pocket is stitched to the underlap. The two short lines of stitching may be joined by another line so as to form a triangle of stitching (Fig. 110). Above this stitching, the underlap and the edge of pocket form the two sides of the placket opening.

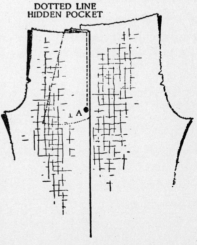

Fig. 112

Lay the other edge of pocket lining along the front edge of the slacks' opening, right sides together, ready to form a plain seam, on the wrong side. The stitching of this seam should lie just (about ⅛″) outside of the seamline of the leg seam. The stitching runs from top of pocket to point A and joins pocket to the one thickness of fabric on the front edge of the opening of the slacks. Fig. 111 shows this seam ready for stitching.

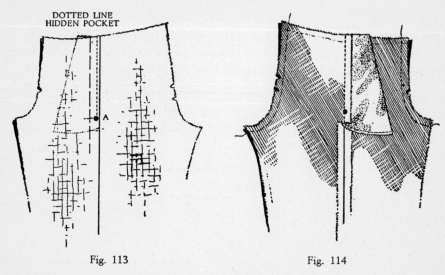

Fig. 113   Fig. 114

Turn the pocket forward into its finished position on the wrong side of slacks. From the right side, baste the folded edge of the front side of the opening so that this edge is in line with the seamline of the leg seam. Surface stitch this fold close to the edge from the top down to point A. The

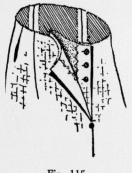

Fig. 115

stitching passes through the surface layer of slacks and through front edge of pocket lining (Fig. 112).

Lay pocket and placket into the position that they will take when slacks are being worn. Baste to hold them in this position and stitch from point A horizontally across the bottom of the opening for ½″ (Fig. 113). The length may be even less than ½″ and a bar tack may be worked over the stitching. This step is to give strength to the lower end of placket and pocket. The bar tack adds a tailored effect.

From the wrong side, stitch together the two sides of the pocket pouch along the curved lower line. Overcast these edges (Fig. 114). Fig. 115 shows the underlap and the one side of the pocket pouch buttoned together as a placket. The mouthline of the pocket is formed by this buttoned edge and the edge of the outer layer of slacks.

PRESSING

If pressing is done after each step in each process, the finished slacks need only a light, final pressing and the addition of the pressed creaseline in the legs.

In general, pressing directions on page 106 may be followed. The light final pressing should be done against the wrong side of the slacks and on only one thickness of fabric. The top of the slacks may be drawn over the end of an ordinary pressing board in order to press a single thickness of fabric. The

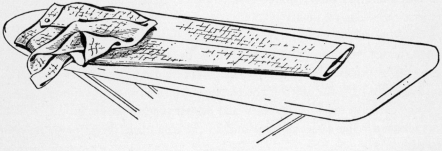

Fig. 116

legs may be drawn over a sleeve board. Since the sleeve board is narrow as well as short, care must be taken to avoid a pressing mark where the fabric has fallen away from the edge of the board. This is not difficult because the leg pressing may be a very light one.

Creaseline in front. Lay the slacks leg folded so that the outer leg seam lies straight and right side down on the board and the inner leg seam coincides with it throughout the length from crotch to hem. The leg seams need not be pressed again.

The creaseline will be indicated by the fold now in place down the front (Fig. 116). It extends from the hem at the bottom to a point about 2″ below the end of the dart in the front. The one dart in front or one of the several will be in line with the creaseline now being pressed. Since the fold of the dart lies flat against the slacks and since the creaseline stands out, the creaseline is not pressed clear up to the end of the dart.

Sometimes, depending on the cut of the pattern and the figure of the wearer, the leg seam near the crotch is so deeply curved that the outer and inner leg seams can coincide only from the hem to the point where the leg seam begins its deepest curve. If that is the case, press the creaseline from the bottom to a point in line with the separation of leg seams and then continue the creaseline upward toward the foldline of dart.

It is possible to overpress the creaseline so that the fabric ripples between the crease and the leg seam. If such ripples do occur, press the rest of the leg between the area just pressed and the leg seam. But even now it is not necessary to re-press the leg seam.

See that the amount of moisture and the degree of pressure applied are the same throughout the length of the creaseline. To do this, it is helpful to have wet and dry press cloths long enough to cover the whole creaseline; to use the "lower-and-lift" motion quickly and lightly several times throughout the length rather than a single firm, heavy motion; to place the iron each time so that the areas pressed overlap each other; to lift the press cloths and release the steam frequently.

Creaselines in back. Place the slacks on the board as they were when the front creases were pressed, except that the back foldline is on the top of the board. Frequently, the two leg seams cannot be made to coincide for a few inches down from the crotch. The reason is the same as it was for the front, but the curve in the back is longer and deeper than in the front.

Press with the same motions and in the same line direction as on the front.

This creaseline ends about 4" below the end of the dart in back. Sometimes, it is in line with this dart. If the back of the slacks has several small darts, usually there will be one that is in line with the creaseline. Some tailors follow a general rule in pressing this crease in men's trousers. The rule is to end it 8" below the top of trousers. This rule is helpful when the back of slacks is cut without a dart.

Watch to see that the crease follows a straight line. Because the crotch seam is a deep curve, you may tend to give the creaseline a curve toward the center back. If you have doubt as to the accuracy of the line, baste the folded edge close to the edge and try on the slacks. It slants slightly toward the center back as a dart does. It should end at the fullest part of the buttocks.

APPEARANCE OF WELL-FITTED SLACKS

Pressing and fitting go hand in hand. The one supplements the other; but neither one can correct errors in the other.

Silhouette lines from a front view are straight lines from hipline to lower hemline of legs. From waistline to hip the fabric lies smooth, but not tight, along the curve of the body. For this reason, a design with pocket-placket combination set in the side seam is not a good choice for a well-rounded or curved hip. A side opening that may be firmly closed is better because it has no loose edges to stand out away from the hipline and thus break the smooth line of silhouette.

Silhouette lines from a side view follow the same principle as above. From waistline to hipline in front, the line follows a slight, smooth curve. From hipline down, the fabric falls in straight lines which are the lines of the creases. In the back, the same is true except that the fabric follows body curves from waistline to the fullest part of the buttocks; then the creaselines fall slightly slanting, but in a straight line, toward the lower hem.

The waistline should be snug and the hipline trim but not snug. Fitting changes are most easily carried out by changing size of darts, either in front or in back. If changed, their direction should still give the effect of a vertical line. Below the end of a dart, the fabric should fall easily without strain. This point is especially noticeable in the front where darts end, not in a point, but in a soft fold like an unstitched tuck. Incorrect fitting may allow for strain and, therefore, a pull against the fabric at the end of the stitching.

If the abdomen is prominent and the waistline small, it may be necessary to alter the center front seam, but it is better to make changes in the darts. The more the center front seam is curved over the abdomen, the fuller the abdomen appears.

In the front, there is a small, soft fold of fabric which falls vertically from center front seam. This fold begins where the crotch seam starts to curve most deeply. The fold may be small, but it should be there.

In the back, a fold of fabric falls from the fullest part of the buttocks downward. The creaseline is centered on this fold of fabric. There is no fold falling from the crotch seamline as there is in front.

If the crotch has been accurately measured and the seam properly made, the crotch seamline follows body curves easily. It is comfortable to the wearer; it is not so long that it sags.

The hemline at the bottom of the legs usually falls smoothly around the ankle. Popular styles may vary on this point. Perhaps the lower line lies against the curve of the heel so low that the front will have a break (wrinkle) over the instep. Tailors of custom-made slacks usually prefer the shorter line suggested first.

APPENDIX

BIBLIOGRAPHY

Galbraith, M. E. D., *Ladies' Tailoring Simplified*. London, Sir Isaac Pitman & Son, Ltd., 1937

Mason, Gertrude, *Tailoring for Women*. New York, The Macmillan Co., 1935

Strickland, Gertrude, *A Tailoring Manual*. Minneapolis, Burgess Publishing Co., 1944.

BULLETINS AND PAMPHLETS

Coat Making at Home. U. S. Department of Agriculture, Farmers' Bulletin No. 1894.

Dressmaking Made Easy. McCall Corp.

Sew and Save. The Spool Cotton Co. 1940.

Simplicity Sewing Book. Simplicity Pattern Co., Inc.

Successful Tailoring. Iowa State College.

Tailoring. The Spool Cotton Co. 1945.

The New Butterick Dressmaker. Butterick Publishing Co. 1927.

Vogue's Book of Dressmaking. The Vogue Pattern Company, Condé Nast Publications, Inc. 1942.

ILLUSTRATION GLOSSARY

chalked seam; creaseline: dotted line

canvas or other reinforcement: spotted cross hatch

catstitch, overcasting, felling, padding stitch, tailor basting: thin line, direction
descriptive of stitch

edge of garment: thick line

finished edge: straight thick line

folded fabric: shaded line

lining: stippled

machine stitch: short spaced line, heavier than hand stitch

tape: thin edge, vertical spotted lines

unfinished edge: uneven dotted line

wool fabric, right side: plain

wool fabric, wrong side: diagonal, left-to-right downward, stroke

zigzag stitching: machine stitch, angular

GLOSSARY

bar tack: a bar made of short strands of thread, closely worked over with stitches crosswise of the bar. It is used to reinforce the end of a placket opening or a pocket mouth-line (Fig. 117).

Fig. 117

beeswax: a wax used to keep thread from curling and knotting.

bias, true: a cut of fabric which is the exact diagonal of a square whose sides are formed by warp and filling yarns (Fig. 118).

bias, garment or long: a cut of fabric which lies between the lines of a true bias and those of warp or filling yarns (Fig. 118, lines A-D).

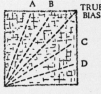

Fig. 118

canvas: a linen or cotton fabric of heavy firm weave, used to reinforce coat collar.

catstitch: a stitch formed by threads crossing so as to hold together two pieces of fabric flatly and smoothly. Threads are slightly slack so that the two pieces of fabric are not held rigidly (Fig. 119).

Fig. 119

clipping seam edges: cutting from raw edge toward stitching lines of seam so as to allow seam edges to lie flat

cotton felt: a material similar to cotton sheet wadding but firmer and heavier.

creaseline of collar: the line along which the collar is folded (Fig. 120).

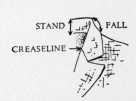

Fig. 120

diagonal basting: see *tailor basting*.

fall of collar: the outside of the collar; the section that falls from creaseline to outer edge of collar (Fig. 120).

felling: a tailor's term for hemming. Some tailors say felling stitches are taken in a direction opposite to that for hemming. In these directions, it indicates a fine firm type of hemming.

171

gimp: a fine cordlike thread that is used to reinforce worked buttonholes.

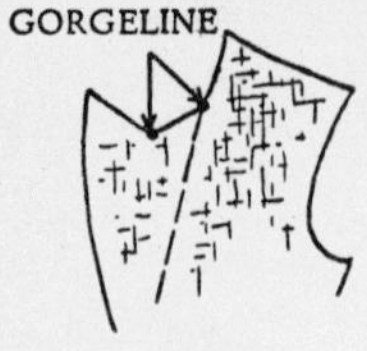

GORGELINE

Fig. 121

gorgeline: a part of the seamline which joins collar to coat. It begins at the point where the jacket neckline crosses the creaseline of the lapel and extends to the end of the collar. Therefore, it is the seamline that joins collar to facing, running from creaseline to notch (Fig. 121). See *notch*.

grading seam edges: trimming one edge of seam shorter than the other, so as to distribute thickness. The longer seam edge should, after pressing, lie against the outside surface of the coat.

ham cushion: a pressing cushion, shaped like a ham, to provide a curved surface needed for shaping.

hymo: a linen and mohair fabric used for reinforcement of body of coat. There are various fabrics similar to hymo which may be satisfactory.

inside of seamlines: a term used here to indicate the area of fabric that lies inside of the stitching line of a seam, farther from the cut edge than is the stitching line. See *outside of seamlines*.

interlining: used in this text as a material inserted between coat and lining to provide extra warmth. There are many types of material available under this name.

mitering: removal of bulk in facing or hem in the turning of a corner.

melton: thick, smooth, twilled woolen fabric, heavier than broadcloth, and resembling felt; used for undercollar because it has firmness and does not fray.

mouthline: see list of terms under *pockets*.

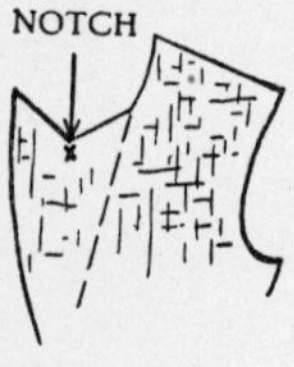

NOTCH

Fig. 122

notch: a term used here, unless otherwise indicated, to define the point at which the front of the collar ends. Also, it is the point of the angle in a notched lapel and collar design. It is one end of the gorgeline (Fig. 122). See also *gorgeline*.

outside of seamlines: the area between the raw edge of a seam and the line of stitching of the seam. See *inside of seamlines*.

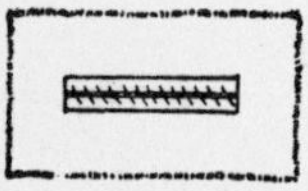

Fig. 123

overcasting: a term with two meanings. Commonly, it is the stitch used to finish a raw edge to keep it from fraying. Often it is a stitch used to hold together two edges which lie flat and yet meet each other. Examples are overcasting the edges of a bound buttonhole or of a pocket mouthline to prevent their separating during subsequent steps in construction (Fig. 123).

padding stitch, or *padding*: used to join two pieces of fabric firmly but not rigidly when one fabric is laid on top of the other. It is worked with the wrong side of the fabric up. A short stitch holds the two layers of fabric together, but it is taken only part way through the thickness of the under fabric. The succeeding short stitches are parallel to it, ½″ or less away from it. When several rows of padding are finished, the thread lies on the surface of the upper layer of fabric in diagonal lines, but no thread shows on the surface of the underlayer (Fig. 124).

Fig. 124

pocket stay: see list of terms under *pockets*.

reinforcement: a fabric such as hymo, used to give body to fabric and to help to hold the shape of the garment.

rolling seam to underside: a term used here to indicate treatment of a finished edge resulting from stitching together two pieces of fabric, as the finished edge of a lapel; the stitching line of the seam lies, not in the center of the bulky edge, but slightly toward the underside. During the process of rolling the seam, the thumbs are placed against the underside (Fig. 125).

Fig. 125

silesia: closely woven, lightweight, smoothly finished, twilled cotton; used for pouches of pockets and to reinforce areas under buttonholes.

stab stitch: a stitch made by pushing the needle down through the fabric and, in a separate motion, up through the fabric. Each time the needle is pushed through at right angles to the fabric. Such a stitch holds layers of bulky materials together without allowing them to draw away from each other or to slide one upon the other.

stand of collar: the part of the collar that stands up against the neck, between the neckline and the creaseline (Fig. 120).

stiletto: a small pointed tool used as a punch in embroidering; used in tailoring to shape a sharp angle at corner of lapel or to make eyelet in worked buttonhole.

surface stitch: often called top stitch, a machine stitch which shows from the right side of the fabric.

swingtack: used to hold one fabric near another, as lining to coat at the hem. A short stitch is taken in each fabric, but ¼″ or more of thread is left between the fabrics. This is repeated to form a bar which is tightly wound with thread (Fig. 126).

Fig. 126

tailor basting: used to hold two layers of fabric together temporarily, as shaped reinforcement and shaped coat front. Short stitches are taken through both layers in a series of parallel lines; the stitches are 1″ to 3″ apart, and thus leave long diagonal threads showing on one side. This is like the pad-

Fig. 127

ding stitch, but is coarser and temporary. Diagonal basting may be done in the same way as tailor basting, but the stitches are shorter (Fig. 127).

tailor's chalk: a fine chalk in a flat cake, that makes a temporary mark easily removed.

Fig. 128a   Fig. 128b

tailor tacks: a temporary marking made with thread as on dart or seamlines. A very short stitch with double thread is taken through two layers of fabric; a second stitch is taken in the same place but the thread is left to form a loop about ½" long. The two layers of fabric may be pulled apart, and the looped threads cut so as to leave cut ends of thread on each layer of fabric (Figs. 128a, b).

Fig. 129

thread marks: a quick method of transferring markings. The marks pull out readily and therefore are very temporary. To make them, take a stitch with double thread through the fabric within the hole of the perforation in the pattern; leave thread loose and take another stitch within the next perforation to be marked. Repeat as needed along a length of line to be marked. Clip the long, loose threads lying on top of pattern. Remove pattern (Fig. 129).

wax chalk: waxy chalk in a flat cake, useful for marking wool when the mark should not rub off easily. Since the mark is removable with a warm iron, the chalk may be used on the right side of wool fabric. If used too heavily, it leaves a spot. The spot may be removed by inserting blotting paper under it and pressing with a warm iron.

welt: see list of terms under *pockets.*

Fig. 130

zigzagging or zigzag stitching: a machine stitch used to join two pieces of fabric with raw edges lapped. It produces a flat joining and prevents raveling of raw edges. It may be done on standard types of machines by removing the screw cap at the top of the presser bar so that the fabric may be drawn forward or backward under the presser foot. Machines that have a backstitching adjustment provide for such stitching (Fig. 130).

INDEX